MW01148639

Daily Morning Prayer: Rite I

Preces (S1)

CD I   TRACK 1

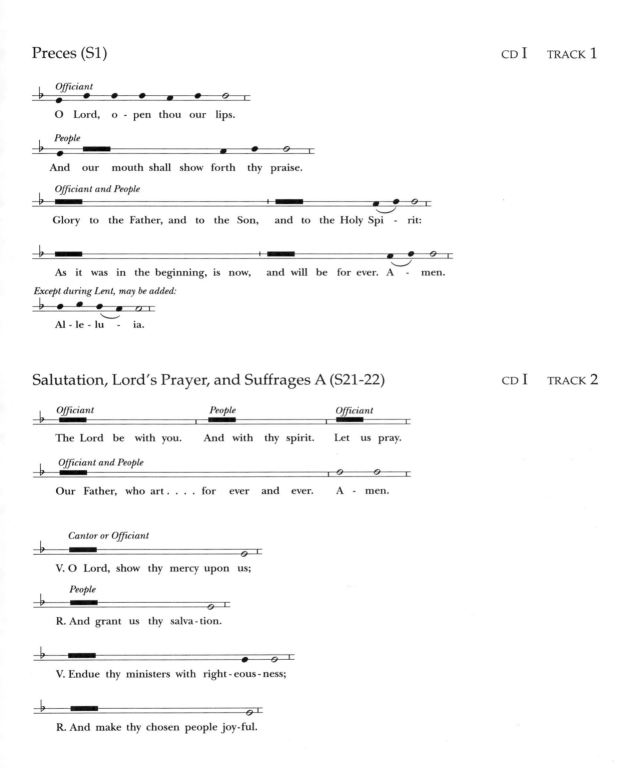

Officiant

O Lord, o - pen thou our lips.

People

And our mouth shall show forth thy praise.

Officiant and People

Glory to the Father, and to the Son, and to the Holy Spi - rit:

As it was in the beginning, is now, and will be for ever. A - men.

Except during Lent, may be added:

Al - le - lu - ia.

Salutation, Lord's Prayer, and Suffrages A (S21-22)

CD I   TRACK 2

Officiant   *People*   *Officiant*

The Lord be with you.   And with thy spirit.   Let us pray.

Officiant and People

Our Father, who art . . . . for ever and ever. A - men.

Cantor or Officiant

V. O Lord, show thy mercy upon us;

People

R. And grant us thy salva - tion.

V. Endue thy ministers with right - eous - ness;

R. And make thy chosen people joy - ful.

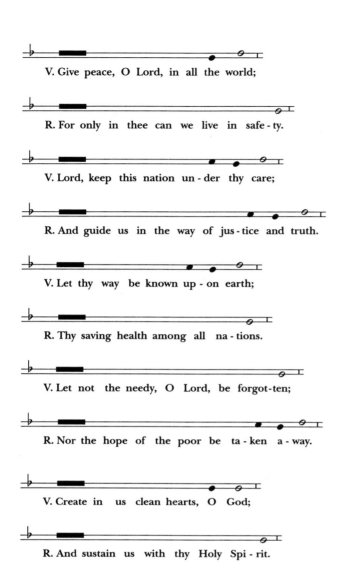

V. Give peace, O Lord, in all the world;

R. For only in thee can we live in safe-ty.

V. Lord, keep this nation un-der thy care;

R. And guide us in the way of jus-tice and truth.

V. Let thy way be known up-on earth;

R. Thy saving health among all na-tions.

V. Let not the needy, O Lord, be forgot-ten;

R. Nor the hope of the poor be ta-ken a-way.

V. Create in us clean hearts, O God;

R. And sustain us with thy Holy Spi-rit.

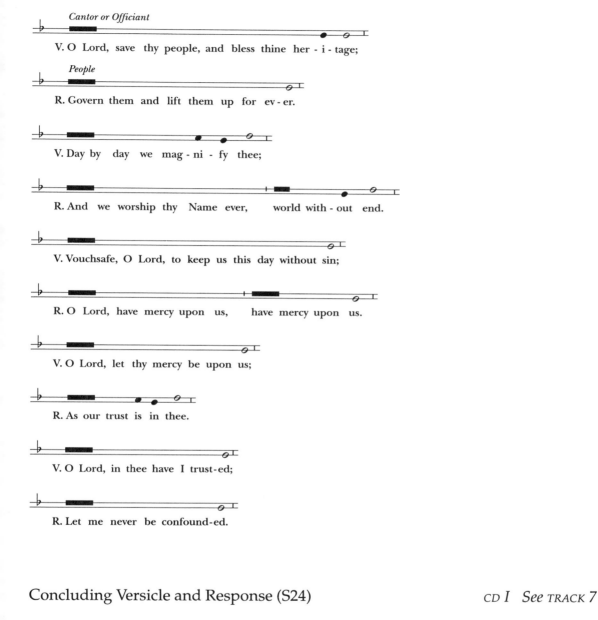

Concluding Versicle and Response (S24)

CD I See TRACK 7

Concluding Versicle and Response in Easter Season (S25)

CD I See TRACK 8

DAILY EVENING PRAYER: RITE I

Preces (S26)

CD I   TRACK 4

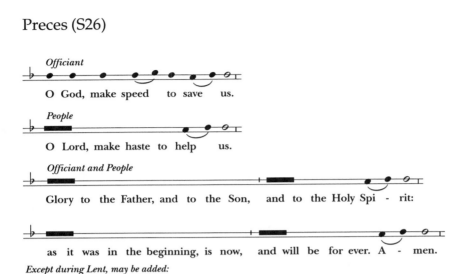

Officiant

O God, make speed to save us.

People

O Lord, make haste to help us.

Officiant and People

Glory to the Father, and to the Son, and to the Holy Spi - rit:

as it was in the beginning, is now, and will be for ever. A - men.

Except during Lent, may be added:

Al - le - lu - ia.

Salutation and the Lord's Prayer Suffrages B, Tone I (S28-29)

CD I   TRACK 5

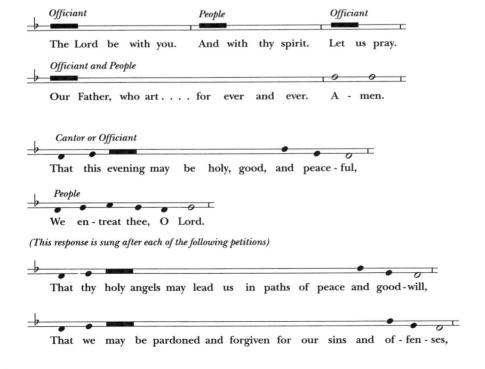

Officiant   *People*   *Officiant*

The Lord be with you.   And with thy spirit.   Let us pray.

Officiant and People

Our Father, who art . . . . for ever and ever. A - men.

Cantor or Officiant

That this evening may be holy, good, and peace - ful,

People

We en - treat thee, O Lord.

(This response is sung after each of the following petitions)

That thy holy angels may lead us in paths of peace and good - will,

That we may be pardoned and forgiven for our sins and of - fen - ses,

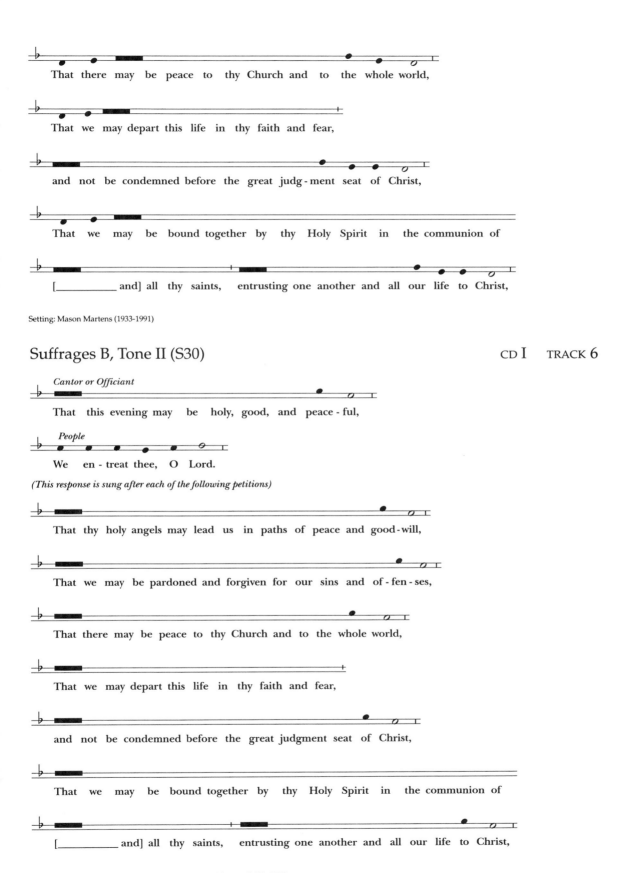

That there may be peace to thy Church and to the whole world,

That we may depart this life in thy faith and fear,

and not be condemned before the great judg-ment seat of Christ,

That we may be bound together by thy Holy Spirit in the communion of

[_____ and] all thy saints, entrusting one another and all our life to Christ,

Setting: Mason Martens (1933-1991)

Suffrages B, Tone II (S30)

CD I   TRACK 6

Cantor or Officiant

That this evening may be holy, good, and peace-ful,

People

We en-treat thee, O Lord.

(This response is sung after each of the following petitions)

That thy holy angels may lead us in paths of peace and good-will,

That we may be pardoned and forgiven for our sins and of-fen-ses,

That there may be peace to thy Church and to the whole world,

That we may depart this life in thy faith and fear,

and not be condemned before the great judgment seat of Christ,

That we may be bound together by thy Holy Spirit in the communion of

[_____ and] all thy saints, entrusting one another and all our life to Christ,

Setting: From the Litany of the Saints; adapt. Mason Martens (1933-1991)

Concluding Versicle and Response (S31)

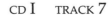

Cantor or Officiant

Let us bless the Lord.

People

Thanks be to God.

Concluding Versicle and Response in Easter (S32)

CD I   TRACK 8

Cantor or Officiant

Let us bless the Lord, al - le - lu - ia,   al - le - lu - ia.

People

Thanks be to God, al - le - lu - ia,   al - le - lu - ia.

DAILY MORNING PRAYER: RITE II

Preces (S33)

CD I   TRACK 9

Officiant

Lord, o - pen our lips.

People

And our mouth shall pro - claim your praise.

Officiant and People

Glory to the Father, and to the Son,   and to the Holy Spi - rit:

As it was in the beginning, is now,   and will be for ever. A - men.

Except in Lent, add:

Al - le - lu - ia.

Salutation, Lord's Prayer, & Suffrages A (S56-58)

CD I   TRACK 10

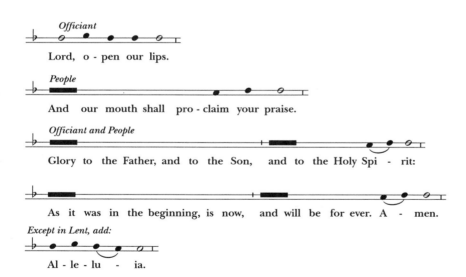

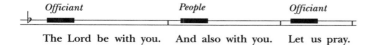

Officiant   *People*   *Officiant*

The Lord be with you.   And also with you.   Let us pray.

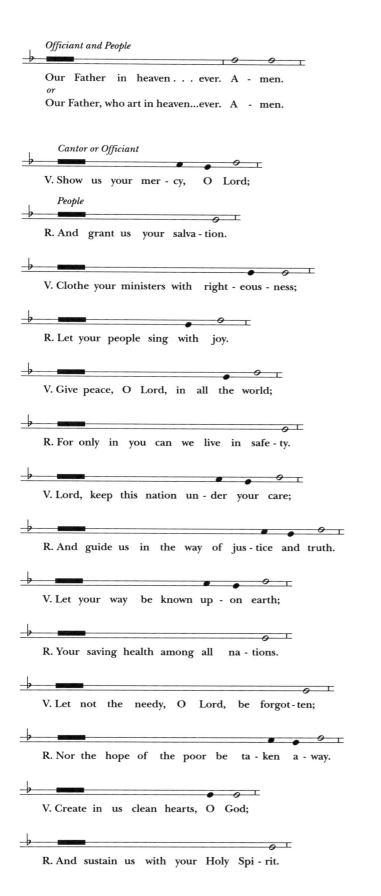

Officiant and People

Our Father in heaven . . . ever. A - men.
or
Our Father, who art in heaven...ever. A - men.

Cantor or Officiant

V. Show us your mer - cy, O Lord;

People

R. And grant us your salva - tion.

V. Clothe your ministers with right - eous - ness;

R. Let your people sing with joy.

V. Give peace, O Lord, in all the world;

R. For only in you can we live in safe - ty.

V. Lord, keep this nation un - der your care;

R. And guide us in the way of jus - tice and truth.

V. Let your way be known up - on earth;

R. Your saving health among all na - tions.

V. Let not the needy, O Lord, be forgot - ten;

R. Nor the hope of the poor be ta - ken a - way.

V. Create in us clean hearts, O God;

R. And sustain us with your Holy Spi - rit.

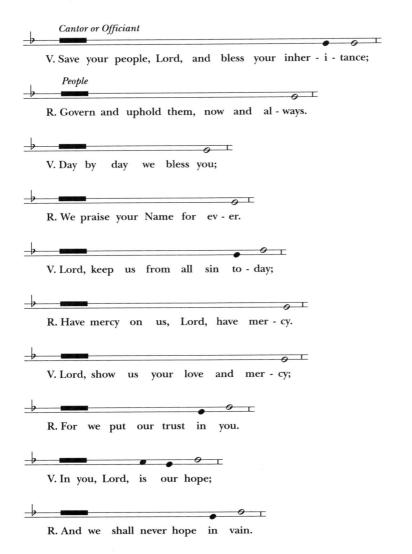

V. Save your people, Lord, and bless your inher - i - tance;

R. Govern and uphold them, now and al - ways.

V. Day by day we bless you;

R. We praise your Name for ev - er.

V. Lord, keep us from all sin to - day;

R. Have mercy on us, Lord, have mer - cy.

V. Lord, show us your love and mer - cy;

R. For we put our trust in you.

V. In you, Lord, is our hope;

R. And we shall never hope in vain.

Concluding Versicle and Response (S54)   CD I   See TRACK 7

Concluding Versicle and Response in Easter Season (S55)   CD I   See TRACK 8

Noonday Prayer

Preces (S296)

CD I TRACK 12

Officiant
O God, make speed to save us. *People* O Lord, make haste to help us.

Officiant and People
Glory to the Father, and to the Son, and to the Holy Spi - rit:

as it was in the beginning, is now, and will be for ever. A - men.

Except in Lent, add

Al - le - lu - ia.

Lord have mercy, Contemporary Lord's Prayer, & Dismissal (S304) CD I TRACK 13

The Officiant then begins the Prayers.

Officiant Lord, have mercy. *People* Christ, have mercy. *Officiant and People* Lord, have mer - cy.

Officiant and People
Our Father in heaven . . . deliver us from e - vil.
or
Our Father, who art in heaven . . . deliver us from e - vil.

Officiant Lord, hear our prayer; *People* And let our cry come to you. *Officiant* Let us pray.

The Officiant then sings one of the Collects appointed. If desired, the Collect of the Day may be used. The Collect may be monotoned or sung to Collect Tone II, S 448.

Free intercessions may be offered.

The service concludes as follows.

Officiant Let us bless the Lord. *People* Thanks be to God.

Noonday setting: Ver. *Hymnal 1982*

ORDER OF WORSHIP FOR THE EVENING & DAILY EVENING PRAYER: RITE II

Greeting, Tone I, Tone II, & Preces (S56-58)

CD I   TRACK 14

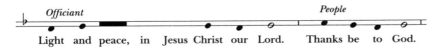

In Lent and in Easter Season, the Opening Acclamations S 78–S 83 are used instead.

Setting: Ambrosian chant; adapt. Mason Martens (1933-1991)

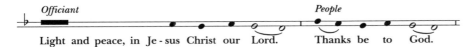

In Lent and in Easter Season, the Opening Acclamations S 78–S 83 are used instead.

Suffrages A

CD I   *See* TRACK 10

Suffrages B, Tone I (S63)

CD I   TRACK 15

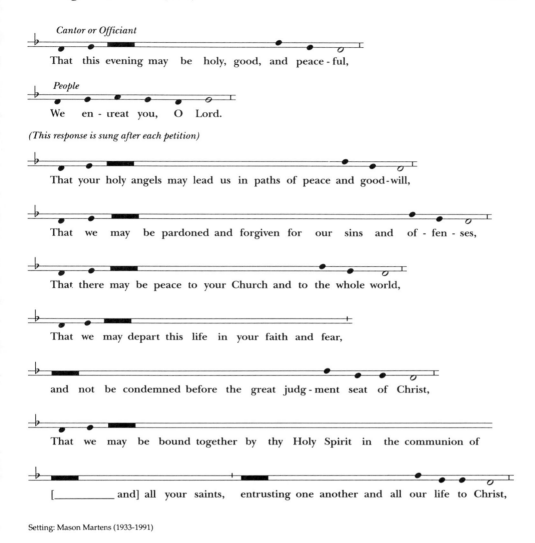

Cantor or Officiant

That this evening may be holy, good, and peace - ful,

People

We en - treat you, O Lord.

(This response is sung after each petition)

That your holy angels may lead us in paths of peace and good - will,

That we may be pardoned and forgiven for our sins and of - fen - ses,

That there may be peace to your Church and to the whole world,

That we may depart this life in your faith and fear,

and not be condemned before the great judg - ment seat of Christ,

That we may be bound together by thy Holy Spirit in the communion of

[_____ and] all your saints, entrusting one another and all our life to Christ,

Setting: Mason Martens (1933-1991)

11

Suffrages B, Tone II (S64)

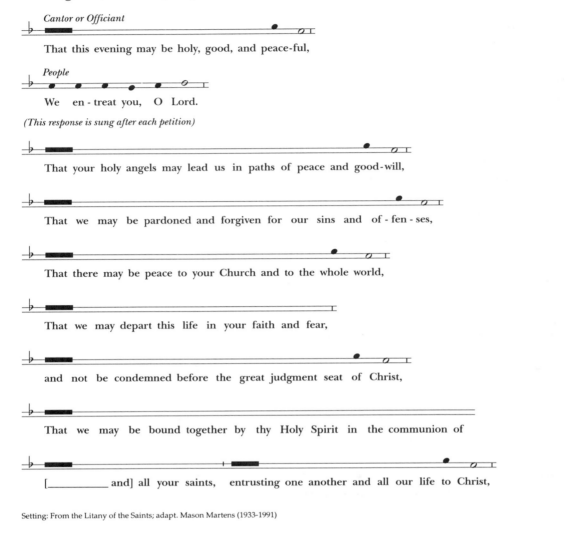

Cantor or Officiant

That this evening may be holy, good, and peace-ful,

People

We en-treat you, O Lord.

(This response is sung after each petition)

That your holy angels may lead us in paths of peace and good-will,

That we may be pardoned and forgiven for our sins and of-fen-ses,

That there may be peace to your Church and to the whole world,

That we may depart this life in your faith and fear,

and not be condemned before the great judgment seat of Christ,

That we may be bound together by thy Holy Spirit in the communion of

[_____ and] all your saints,   entrusting one another and all our life to Christ,

Setting: From the Litany of the Saints; adapt. Mason Martens (1933-1991)

Concluding Versicle and Response (S65)

CD I   *See* TRACK 7

Concluding Versicle and Response in Easter Season (S66)

CD I   *See* TRACK 8

COMPLINE

Preces (S321)　　　　　　　　　　　　　　　　　　CD I　　TRACK 17

Officiant
The Lord Almighty grant us a peace-ful night and a

per-fect end. *People* A-men.

Officiant Our help is in the name of the Lord; *People* The maker of heaven and earth.

Officiant O God, make speed to save us. *People* O Lord, make haste to help us.

Officiant and People Glory to the Father, and to the Son, and to the Holy Spi-rit:

as it was in the beginning, is now, and will be for ever. A-men.

Except in Lent, add:
Al-le-lu-ia.

Responsory, Versicles and Prayers (Elaborate) (S331, 333, 334)　　CD I　　TRACK 18

Officiant or Cantor
In-to your hands, O Lord, I com-mend my spi-rit.

People
In-to your hands, O Lord, I com-mend my spi-rit.

Officiant or Cantor
For you have re-deemed me, O Lord, O God of truth.

People
In-to your hands, O Lord, I com-mend my spi-rit.

V. Keep us, O Lord, as the apple of your eye;

R. Hide us under the shadow of your wings.

Lord, have mercy. Christ, have mercy. Lord, have mer-cy.

Our Father in heaven . . . deliver us from e-vil.

or

Our Father, who art in heaven . . . deliver us from e-vil.

Lord, hear our prayer; And let our cry come to you.

Let us pray.

Responsory, Versicles, and Prayers (Simple) (S332, 333, 335)　　CD I　TRACK 19

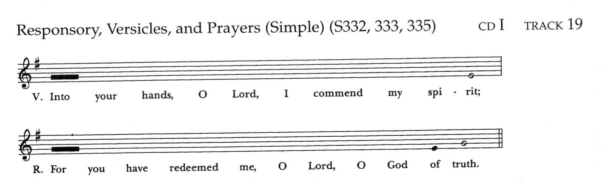

V. Into your hands, O Lord, I commend my spi-rit;

R. For you have redeemed me, O Lord, O God of truth.

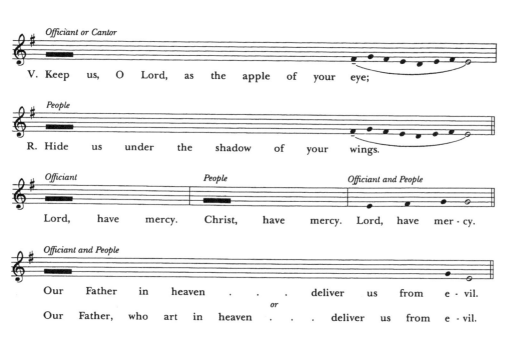

V. Keep us, O Lord, as the apple of your eye;

R. Hide us under the shadow of your wings.

Lord, have mercy. Christ, have mercy. Lord, have mer-cy.

Our Father in heaven . . . deliver us from e-vil.

or

Our Father, who art in heaven . . . deliver us from e-vil.

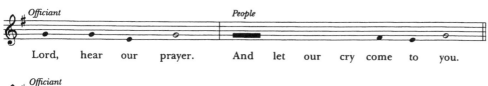

Lord, hear our prayer. And let our cry come to you.

Let us pray.

Concluding Versicle and Blessing (S337)

CD I   TRACK 20

Let us bless the Lord. Thanks be to God.

The almighty and mer-ci-ful Lord, Father, Son, and Holy Spi-rit,

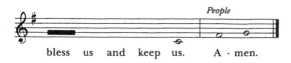

bless us and keep us. A-men.

Compline Setting: adapt. David Hurd (b. 1950)

The Great Litany (S67)

The Officiant at the Litany may be a lay cantor.

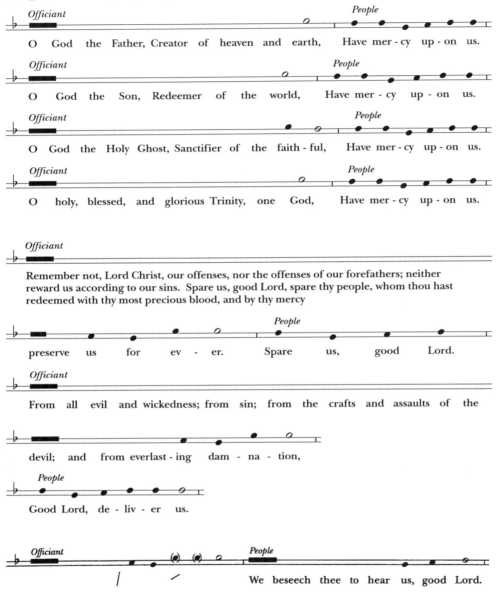

Officiant

O God the Father, Creator of heaven and earth,

People

Have mer - cy up - on us.

Officiant

O God the Son, Redeemer of the world,

People

Have mer - cy up - on us.

Officiant

O God the Holy Ghost, Sanctifier of the faith - ful,

People

Have mer - cy up - on us.

Officiant

O holy, blessed, and glorious Trinity, one God,

People

Have mer - cy up - on us.

Officiant

Remember not, Lord Christ, our offenses, nor the offenses of our forefathers; neither
reward us according to our sins. Spare us, good Lord, spare thy people, whom thou hast
redeemed with thy most precious blood, and by thy mercy

preserve us for ev - er.

People

Spare us, good Lord.

Officiant

From all evil and wickedness; from sin; from the crafts and assaults of the

devil; and from everlast - ing dam - na - tion,

People

Good Lord, de - liv - er us.

Officiant

People

We beseech thee to hear us, good Lord.

(This same response is sung after the petitions that follow)

We sinners do beseech thee to hear us, O Lord God; and that it may please thee to rule and
govern thy holy Church Universal in the right way,

16

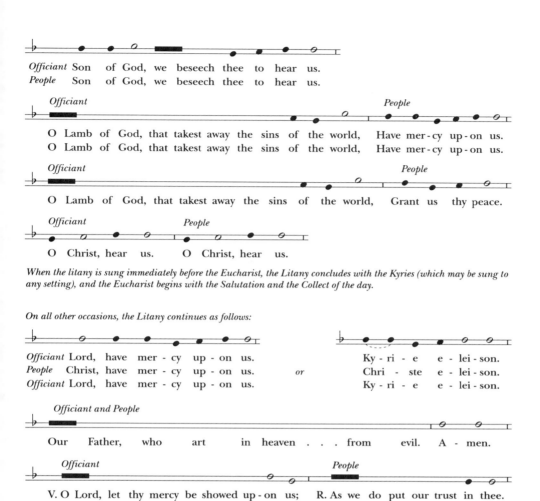

Officiant Son of God, we beseech thee to hear us.
People Son of God, we beseech thee to hear us.

Officiant   People

O Lamb of God, that takest away the sins of the world, Have mer-cy up-on us.
O Lamb of God, that takest away the sins of the world, Have mer-cy up-on us.

Officiant   People

O Lamb of God, that takest away the sins of the world, Grant us thy peace.

Officiant   People

O Christ, hear us. O Christ, hear us.

When the litany is sung immediately before the Eucharist, the Litany concludes with the Kyries (which may be sung to any setting), and the Eucharist begins with the Salutation and the Collect of the day.

On all other occasions, the Litany continues as follows:

Officiant Lord, have mer-cy up-on us.   Ky-ri-e e-lei-son.
People Christ, have mer-cy up-on us.   *or*   Chri-ste e-lei-son.
Officiant Lord, have mer-cy up-on us.   Ky-ri-e e-lei-son.

Officiant and People

Our Father, who art in heaven . . . from evil. A-men.

Officiant   People

V. O Lord, let thy mercy be showed up-on us;   R. As we do put our trust in thee.

The Officiant sings the concluding Collect.

The Supplication – Versicle Tone (S338)

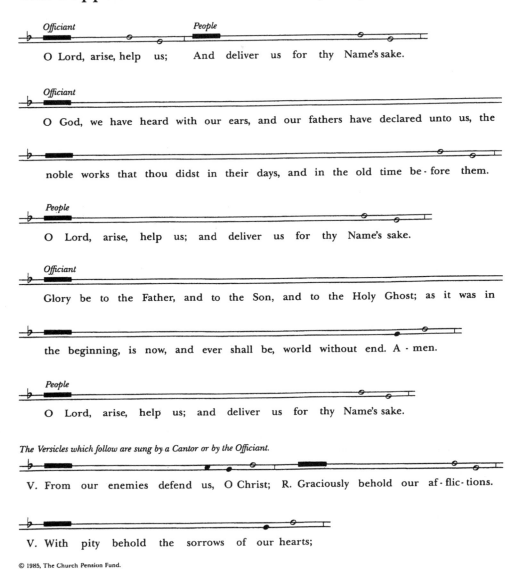

Officiant   *People*

O Lord, arise, help us;   And deliver us for thy Name's sake.

Officiant

O God, we have heard with our ears, and our fathers have declared unto us, the

noble works that thou didst in their days, and in the old time be - fore them.

People

O Lord, arise, help us; and deliver us for thy Name's sake.

Officiant

Glory be to the Father, and to the Son, and to the Holy Ghost; as it was in

the beginning, is now, and ever shall be, world without end. A - men.

People

O Lord, arise, help us; and deliver us for thy Name's sake.

The Versicles which follow are sung by a Cantor or by the Officiant.

V. From our enemies defend us, O Christ;   R. Graciously behold our af - flic - tions.

V. With pity behold the sorrows of our hearts;

© 1985, The Church Pension Fund.

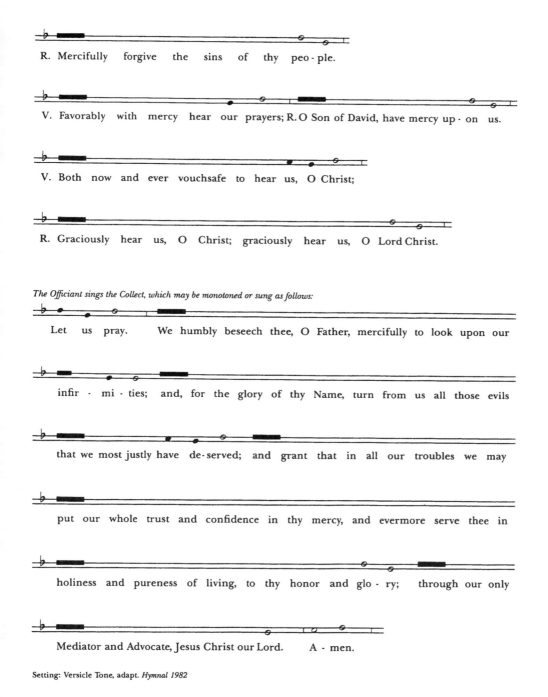

R. Mercifully forgive the sins of thy peo - ple.

V. Favorably with mercy hear our prayers; R. O Son of David, have mercy up - on us.

V. Both now and ever vouchsafe to hear us, O Christ;

R. Graciously hear us, O Christ; graciously hear us, O Lord Christ.

The Officiant sings the Collect, which may be monotoned or sung as follows:

Let us pray. We humbly beseech thee, O Father, mercifully to look upon our

infir - mi - ties; and, for the glory of thy Name, turn from us all those evils

that we most justly have de - served; and grant that in all our troubles we may

put our whole trust and confidence in thy mercy, and evermore serve thee in

holiness and pureness of living, to thy honor and glo - ry; through our only

Mediator and Advocate, Jesus Christ our Lord. A - men.

Setting: Versicle Tone, adapt. *Hymnal 1982*

The Supplication – Mode 4 (S339)

Choir or All

O Lord, a - rise, help us; and deliver us for thy Name's sake.

Cantor

O God, we have heard with our ears, and our fathers

have declared un - to us, the noble works that thou didst

in their days, and in the old time be - fore them.

Choir or All

O Lord, a - rise, help us, and deliver us for thy Name's sake.

Cantor

Glo - ry be to the Father, and to the Son, and to the

Ho - ly Ghost; as it was in the begin - ning, is now, and

ev - er shall be, world with - out end. A - men.

Choir or All

O Lord, a - rise, help us; and deliver us for thy Name's sake.

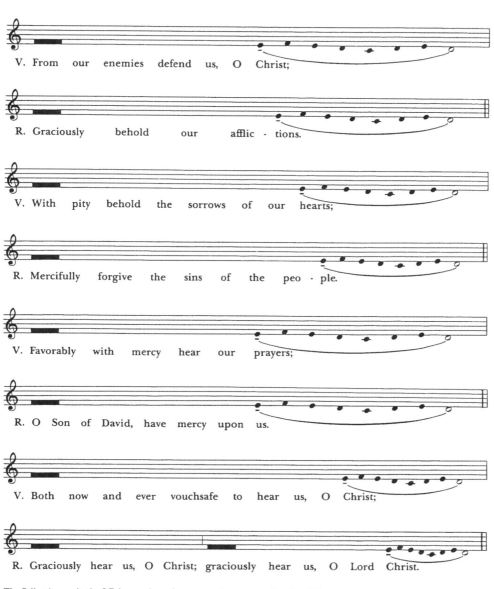

V. From our enemies defend us, O Christ;

R. Graciously behold our afflic - tions.

V. With pity behold the sorrows of our hearts;

R. Mercifully forgive the sins of the peo - ple.

V. Favorably with mercy hear our prayers;

R. O Son of David, have mercy upon us.

V. Both now and ever vouchsafe to hear us, O Christ;

R. Graciously hear us, O Christ; graciously hear us, O Lord Christ.

The Collect is sung by the Officiant, and may be monotoned or sung as given in S 338.

Setting: Mode 4 antiphon melody; adapt. Howard E. Galley (b. 1929)

Palm Sunday Liturgy of the Palms

Anthem, Blessing over the Branches, Anthem. Procession (H153) CD I   TRACK 24

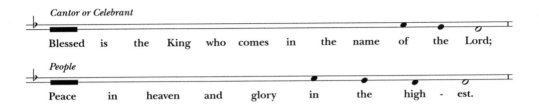

Cantor or Celebrant
Blessed is the King who comes in the name of the Lord;

People
Peace in heaven and glory in the high - est.

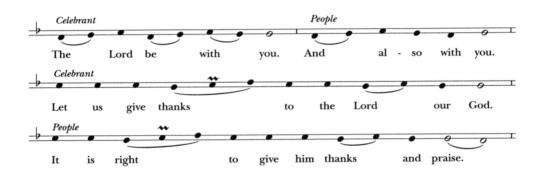

Celebrant
The Lord be with you.

People
And al - so with you.

Celebrant
Let us give thanks to the Lord our God.

People
It is right to give him thanks and praise.

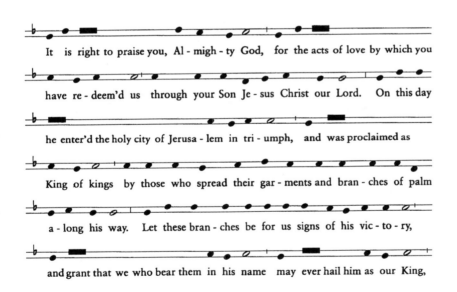

It is right to praise you, Al - migh - ty God, for the acts of love by which you

have re - deem'd us through your Son Je - sus Christ our Lord. On this day

he enter'd the holy city of Jerusa - lem in tri - umph, and was proclaimed as

King of kings by those who spread their gar - ments and bran - ches of palm

a - long his way. Let these bran - ches be for us signs of his vic - to - ry,

and grant that we who bear them in his name may ever hail him as our King,

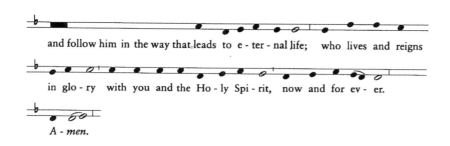

and follow him in the way that leads to e - ter - nal life; who lives and reigns

in glo - ry with you and the Ho - ly Spi - rit, now and for ev - er.

A - men.

Cantor or Celebrant

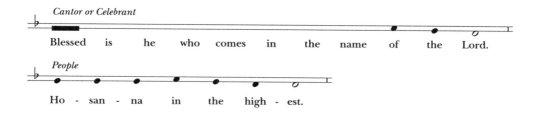

Blessed is he who comes in the name of the Lord.

People

Ho - san - na in the high - est.

Deacon   *People*

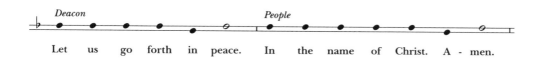

Let us go forth in peace. In the name of Christ. A - men.

GOOD FRIDAY

Acclamation

CD I   TRACK 25

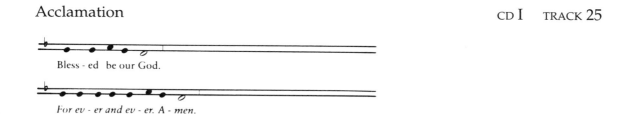

Bless - ed be our God.

For ev - er and ev - er. A - men.

Solemn Collects and Biddings

CD I   TRACK 26

Deacon or leader

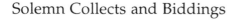

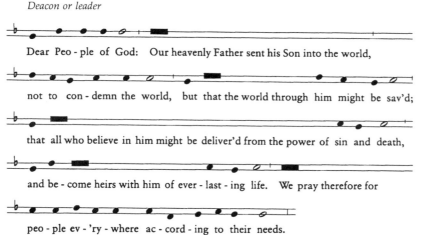

Dear Peo - ple of God: Our heavenly Father sent his Son into the world,

not to con - demn the world, but that the world through him might be sav'd;

that all who believe in him might be deliver'd from the power of sin and death,

and be - come heirs with him of ever - last - ing life. We pray therefore for

peo - ple ev - 'ry - where ac - cord - ing to their needs.

Let us pray for the holy Catholic Church of Christ through-out the world;

For its unity in wit-ness and ser-vice; For all bishops and other ministers

and the people whom they serve; For N., our Bishop, and all the people of this

di-o-cese; For all Chris-tians in this com-mu-ni-ty; For those a-bout

to be bap-tized (particularly _____); That God will confirm his

Church in faith, increase it in love and pre-serve it in peace. * Silence

Deacon or leader

Let us kneel in si-lent prayer. *Silence* A-rise.

Celebrant

Almighty and everlasting God, by whose Spirit the whole body of your

faithful people is gov-ern'd and sanc-ti-fied: Receive our supplications and

prayers which we offer before you for all members of your ho-ly Church,

that in their vocation and ministry they may truly and de-vout-ly serve you;

through our Lord and Savior Je-sus Christ. A-*men*.

Deacon or leader

Let us pray for all nations and peoples of the earth, and for those in authori-ty

a-mong them; For N., the President of the U-ni-ted States; For the Con-gress

and the Supreme Court; For the Members and Representatives of the U-ni-ted

Na-tions; For all who serve the com-mon good; That by God's help they may

seek justice and truth, and live in peace and con-cord. Silence

Celebrant

Al - migh - ty God, kindle, we pray, in every heart the true love of peace,

and guide with your wisdom those who take counsel for the na - tions of the earth;

that in tranquillity your dominion may increase, until the earth is filled with

the know - ledge of your love; through Je - sus Christ our Lord. A - *men*.

Deacon or leader

Let us pray for all who suffer and are afflicted in body or in mind; For the

hungry and the homeless, the destitute and the op - press'd; For the sick, the

wound - ed and the crip - pled; For those in loneliness, fear and an - guish;

For those who face temptation, doubt and de - spair; For the sor - row - ful

and be - reav'd; For prisoners and captives, and those in mor - tal dan - ger;

That God in his mercy will comfort and re - lieve them, and grant them the

knowledge of his love, and stir up in us the will and patience to min - is - ter

to their needs. **Silence**

Celebrant

Gra - cious God, the comfort of all who sorrow, the strength of all who

suf - fer: Let the cry of those in misery and need come to you, that they may

find your mercy present with them in all their af - flic - tions; and give us, we

pray, the strength to serve them for the sake of him who suf - fer'd for us,

your Son Jesus Christ our Lord. A - *men*.

Deacon or leader

Let us pray for all who have not received the Gos - pel of Christ; For those who have never heard the word of sal - va - tion; For those who have lost their faith; For those hardened by sin or in - dif - fer - ence; For the con - temp - tuous and the scorn - ful; For those who are enemies of the cross of Christ and persecutors of his dis - ci - ples; For those who in the name of Christ have perse - cu - ted o - thers; That God will open their hearts to the truth, and lead them to faith and o - be - di - ence.   Silence

Celebrant

Mer - ci - ful God, Creator of all the peoples of the earth and lov - er of souls: Have compassion on all who do not know you as you are revealed in your Son Je - sus Christ;   let your Gospel be preached with grace and power to those who have not heard it;   turn the hearts of those who resist it;   and bring home to your fold those who have gone a - stray;   that there may be one flock under one shep - herd, Je - sus Christ our Lord.   A - *men.*

Deacon or leader

Let us commit ourselves to our God, and pray for the grace of a ho - ly life, that with all who have departed this world and have died in the peace of Christ, and those whose faith is known to God a - lone, we may be accounted worthy to enter into the fullness of the joy of our Lord, and receive the crown of life in the day of re - sur - rec - tion.   Silence

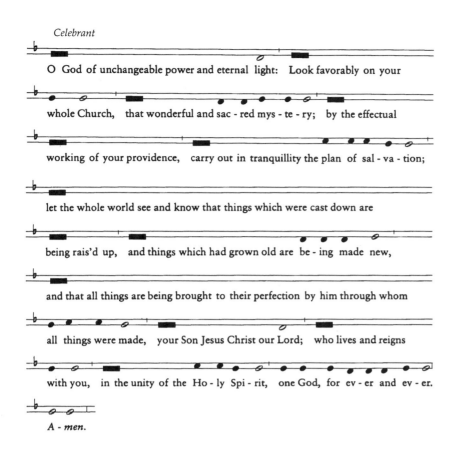

O God of unchangeable power and eternal light: Look favorably on your whole Church, that wonderful and sac - red mys - te - ry; by the effectual working of your providence, carry out in tranquillity the plan of sal - va - tion; let the whole world see and know that things which were cast down are being rais'd up, and things which had grown old are be - ing made new, and that all things are being brought to their perfection by him through whom all things were made, your Son Jesus Christ our Lord; who lives and reigns with you, in the unity of the Ho - ly Spi - rit, one God, for ev - er and ev - er.

A - men.

Final Prayer

CD I TRACK 27

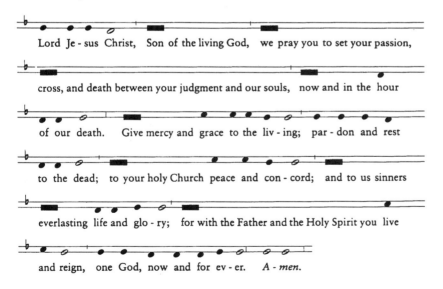

Lord Je - sus Christ, Son of the living God, we pray you to set your passion, cross, and death between your judgment and our souls, now and in the hour of our death. Give mercy and grace to the liv - ing; par - don and rest to the dead; to your holy Church peace and con - cord; and to us sinners everlasting life and glo - ry; for with the Father and the Holy Spirit you live and reign, one God, now and for ev - er. A - men.

THE GREAT VIGIL OF EASTER

The Light of Christ (S68)

CD I   TRACK 28

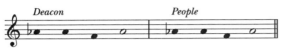

The light of Christ. Thanks be to God.

At the second and third pause, the Versicle and Response is sung successively a step higher.

Exsultet

CD I   TRACK 29

Re-joice now, heav'n-ly hosts and choirs of an-gels,

and let your trum-pets shout Sal-va-tion

for the vic-to-ry of our migh-ty King.

Re-joice and sing now, all the round earth,

bright with a glo-ri-ous splen-dor,

for dark-ness has been van-quish'd by our e-ter-nal King.

Re-joice and be glad now, Mo-ther Church,

and let your ho-ly courts in ra-diant light

re-sound with the prais-es of your peo-ple.

[All you who stand near this mar-ve-lous and ho-ly flame,

pray with me to God the Al - migh - ty

for the grace to sing the wor - thy praise of this great light;

through Je - sus Christ his Son our Lord,

who lives and reigns with him,

in the u - ni - ty of the Ho - ly Spi - rit, one God,

for ev - er and ev - er.   A - men.]

Deacon

The Lord be with you.

People

And al - so with you.

Deacon

Let us give thanks to the Lord our God.

People

It is right to give him thanks and praise.

It is tru - ly right and good, al - ways and ev - 'ry - where,

with our whole heart and mind and voice to praise you,

the in - vi - si - ble, al - migh - ty and e - ter - nal God,

and your on - ly - be - got - ten Son Je - sus Christ our Lord;

for he is the true Pas - chal Lamb, who at the feast of the Pass - o - ver

paid for us the debt of A - dam's sin,

and by his blood de - liv - er'd your faith - ful peo - ple.

This is the night, when you brought our fa - thers,

the chil - dren of Is - ra - el, out of bon - dage in E - gypt,

and led them through the Red Sea on dry land.

This is the night, when all who be - lieve in Christ

are de - liv - er'd from the gloom of sin,

and are re - stor'd to grace and ho - li - ness of life.

This is the night,

when Christ broke the bonds of death and hell,

and rose vic - to - rious from the grave.

[How won - der - ful and be - yond our know - ing, O God, is your

mer - cy and lov - ing — kind - ness to us, that to re - deem a slave,

you gave a Son. How ho - ly is this night, when wick - ed -

ness is put to flight, and sin is wash'd a - way. It re - stores in -

no - cence to the fall - en, and joy to those who mourn. It casts out

pride and ha - tred, and brings peace and con - cord. How bless - ed

is this night, when earth and hea - ven are joined and man

is re - con - cil'd to God.]

Ho - ly Fa - ther, ac - cept our ev - 'ning sac - ri - fice,

the of - fer - ing of this can - dle in your ho - nor.

May it shine con - tin - ual - ly to drive a - way all dark - ness.

May Christ, the Morn - ing Star who knows no set - ting,

find it ev - er burn - ing —

he who gives his light to all cre - a - tion,

and who lives and reigns for ev - er and ev - er. A - men.

Great Alleluia (S70)

CD I   TRACK 30

After the Epistle, this Alleluia is traditionally sung three times by the Celebrant or by a Cantor, at successively higher pitches (one whole tone each time), the Congregation repeating it each time.

Al - le - - - lu - ia.

HOLY BAPTISM

Opening Acclamation CD I   *See TRACK 36*

Opening Acclamation in Easter Season CD I   *See TRACK 38*

Opening Acclamation in Lent (Rite I) CD I   *See TRACK 40*

Opening Acclamation in Lent (Rite II) CD I   *See TRACK 42*

Versicles (S74)

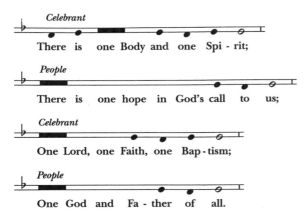

Celebrant
There is one Body and one Spi - rit;

People
There is one hope in God's call to us;

Celebrant
One Lord, one Faith, one Bap - tism;

People
One God and Fa - ther of all.

Setting: Ambrosian chant; adapt. *Hymnal 1982*

Prayers for the Candidates (S75)

Deliver *them*, O Lord, from the way | of sín and death.	*Lord, hear our prayer.*
Open *their hearts* to | your gráce and truth.	*Lord, hear our prayer.*
Fill *them* with your holy and life-giv - | ing Spí - rit.	*Lord, hear our prayer.*
Keep *them* in the faith and communion of | your hó - ly Church.	*Lord, hear our prayer.*
Teach *them* to love others in the power of | the Spí - rit.	*Lord, hear our prayer.*
Send *them* into the world in wit - | ness tó your love.	*Lord, hear our prayer.*
Bring *them* to the fullness of your peace | and gló - ry.	*Lord, hear our prayer.*

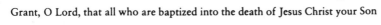

Grant, O Lord, that all who are baptized into the death of Jesus Christ your Son

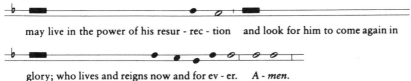

may live in the power of his resur - rec - tion and look for him to come again in

glory; who lives and reigns now and for ev - er. A - *men*.

Thanksgiving over the Water

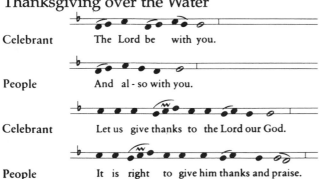

Celebrant   The Lord be with you.

People   And al - so with you.

Celebrant   Let us give thanks to the Lord our God.

People   It is right to give him thanks and praise.

We thank you, Almighty God, for the gift of wa - ter. Ov - er it the Holy Spirit mov'd in the beginning of cre - a - tion. Through it you led the children of Israel out of their bon - dage in E - gypt in - to the land of pro - mise. In it your Son Jesus receiv'd the Bap - tism of John and was anointed by the Holy Spirit as the Mes - si - ah, the Christ, to lead us, through his death and re - sur - rec - tion, from the bon - dage of sin in - to ev - er - last - ing life. We thank you, Fa - ther, for the wa - ter of Bap - tism. In it we are buried with Christ in his death. By it we share in his re - sur - rec - tion. Through it we are reborn by the Ho - ly Spi - rit. There - fore in joyful obedience to your Son, we bring into his fellowship those who come to him in faith, baptizing them in the Name of the Father, and of the Son, and of the Ho - ly Spi - rit. Now sanctify this wa - ter, we pray you, by the power of your Ho - ly Spi - rit, that those who here are cleansed from sin and born a - gain may continue for ever in the ris - en life of Je - sus Christ our Sa - vior. To him, to you, and to the Ho - ly Spi - rit, be all hon - or and glo - ry, now and for ev - er. A - men.

Consecration of Chrism

CD I TRACK 34

Bishop

E - ternal Father, whose blessed Son was anointed by the Ho - ly Spi - rit to be the Sa - vior and ser - vant of all, we pray you to con - se - crate this oil, that those who are seal'd with it may share in the royal priesthood of Je - sus Christ; who lives and reigns with you and the Ho - ly Spi - rit, for ev - er and ev - er. A - men.

THE HOLY EUCHARIST, RITE I

The Decalogue (S353)

CD I   TRACK 35

God spake these words, and said:
I am the Lord thy God who brought
      thee out of the land of
Egypt, out of the house of bondage.
      Thou shalt have none
other gods but me.

Lord, have mer - cy up - on us, and in - cline our hearts to keep this law.

Thou shalt not make to thyself any
      graven image, nor the
likeness of any thing that is in heaven
      above, or in the earth
beneath, or in the water under the
      earth; thou shalt not bow
down to them, nor worship them.

Lord, have mer - cy up - on us, and write all these thy laws in our

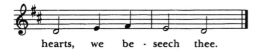

hearts, we be - seech thee.

Setting: From *Missa de Sancta Maria Magdalena*, Healey Willan (1880-1968)
Copyright, 1928, by the Oxford University Press. London. Renewed in U.S.A. 1956.

Opening Acclamation (S76)

CD I   TRACK 36

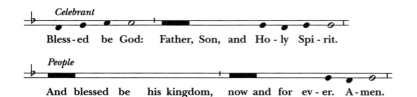

Bless - ed be God: Father, Son, and Ho - ly Spi - rit.

And blessed be his kingdom, now and for ev - er. A - men.

Setting: Ambrosian chant; adapt. Mason Martens (1933-1991)

Opening Acclamation from *Missa orbis factor* (S77)

Celebrant

Bless - ed be God: Fa - ther, Son, and Ho - ly Spi - rit.

People

And bless - ed be his king-dom, now and for ev - er. A - men.

Setting: From *Missa orbis factor*; arr. David Hurd (b.1950)

Opening Acclamation in Easter Season (S78)

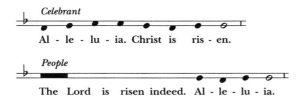

Celebrant

Al - le - lu - ia. Christ is ris - en.

People

The Lord is risen indeed. Al - le - lu - ia.

Setting: Ambrosian chant; adapt. Mason Martens (1933-1991)

Opening Acclamation in Easter Season from *Missa orbis factor* (S79)

Celebrant

Al - le - lu - ia. Christ is ris - en.

People

The Lord is ris - en in - deed. Al - le - lu - ia.

Setting: From *Missa orbis factor*; arr. David Hurd (b.1950)

Opening Acclamation in Lent (Rite I) (S80)

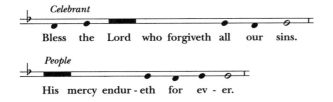

Celebrant

Bless the Lord who forgiveth all our sins.

People

His mercy endur - eth for ev - er.

Setting: Ambrosian chant; adapt. Mason Martens (1933-1991)

Opening Acclamation in Lent (Rite I) from *Missa orbis factor* (S81) CD I TRACK 41

Setting: From *Missa orbis factor*; arr. David Hurd (b.1950)

Opening Acclamation in Lent (Rite II) (S82) CD I TRACK 42

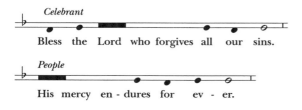

Setting: Ambrosian chant; adapt. Mason Martens (1933-1991)

Opening Acclamation in Lent (Rite II) from *Missa orbis factor* (S83) CD I TRACK 43

Setting: From *Missa orbis factor*; arr. David Hurd (b.1950)

Salutation CD I *See* TRACK 2

Collect, Tone I

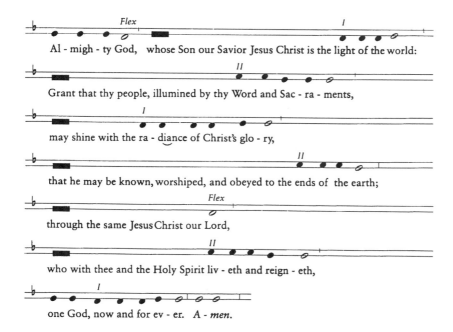

Al - migh - ty God,   whose Son our Savior Jesus Christ is the light of the world:

Grant that thy people, illumined by thy Word and Sac - ra - ments,

may shine with the ra - diance of Christ's glo - ry,

that he may be known, worshiped, and obeyed to the ends of the earth;

through the same Jesus Christ our Lord,

who with thee and the Holy Spirit liv - eth and reign - eth,

one God, now and for ev - er. A - men.

Collect, Tone II

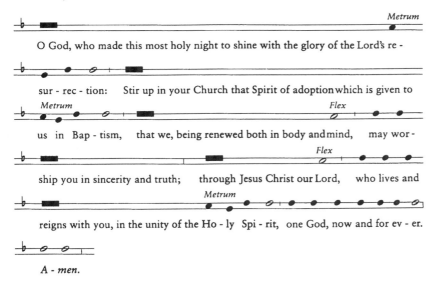

O God, who made this most holy night to shine with the glory of the Lord's re -

sur - rec - tion: Stir up in your Church that Spirit of adoption which is given to

us in Bap - tism,   that we, being renewed both in body and mind,   may wor -

ship you in sincerity and truth;   through Jesus Christ our Lord,   who lives and

reigns with you, in the unity of the Ho - ly Spi - rit, one God, now and for ev - er.

A - men.

Lessons before the Gospel

CD I   TRACK 46

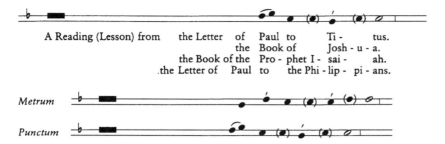

A Reading (Lesson) from   the Letter   of   Paul   to   Ti -   tus.
                           the Book of   Josh - u - a.
                           the Book of the Pro - phet I - sai -   ah.
                           the Letter of   Paul   to   the Phi - lip - pi - ans.

Metrum

Punctum

Colossians 3:1-4

If you have been raised with Christ, seek the things that
are above, where Christ is, seated at the right hand of
God. Set your minds on things that are above, not on
things that are on earth, for you have died, and your life
is hidden with Christ in God. When Christ who is your
life is revealed, then you also will be revealed with him
in glory.

Gospel Tone I

CD I   TRACK 47

The Holy Gospel of our Lord Je - sus Christ   ac - cord - ing to Mat - thew.
                                              Mark.
                                              Luke.
                                              John.

Rite I

Glo - ry be to thee, O Lord.

Rite II

Glo - ry to you, Lord Christ.

Metrum

Punctum

Question

3 2 1

Conclusion

The metrum is used at the end of the first major clause within each sentence. In a very long sentence the metrum may be repeated. In a short sentence, the metrum is omitted.

The punctum is used at the conclusion of each sentence. It may also be used at a colon or semi-colon in a compound sentence in which the metrum has already been used.

Questions are sung a semi-tone lower, concluding with an invariable formula set to the last three syllables. In very long questions the descent of a semi-tone is not made until the last section of the question. Questions of less than four syllables begin on the numbered note corresponding to the number of syllables.

The conclusion is treated rather freely, in accordance with the sense and accentual pattern of the words.

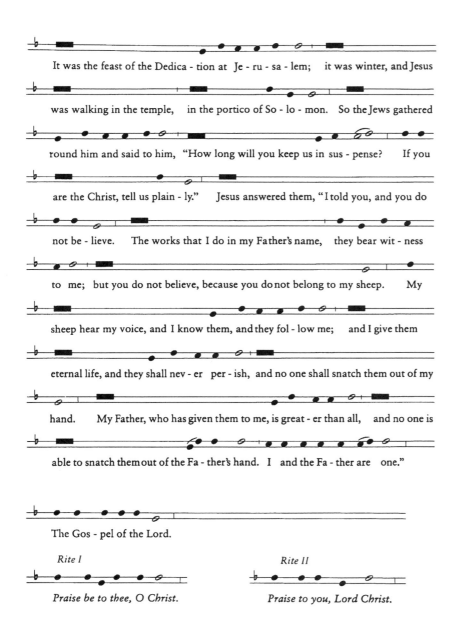

It was the feast of the Dedica - tion at Je - ru - sa - lem;   it was winter, and Jesus was walking in the temple,   in the portico of So - lo - mon.   So the Jews gathered round him and said to him, "How long will you keep us in sus - pense?   If you are the Christ, tell us plain - ly."   Jesus answered them, "I told you, and you do not be - lieve.   The works that I do in my Father's name,   they bear wit - ness to me;   but you do not believe, because you do not belong to my sheep.   My sheep hear my voice, and I know them, and they fol - low me;   and I give them eternal life, and they shall nev - er per - ish,   and no one shall snatch them out of my hand.   My Father, who has given them to me, is great - er than all,   and no one is able to snatch them out of the Fa - ther's hand.   I and the Fa - ther are one."

The Gos - pel of the Lord.

Rite I

Praise be to thee, O Christ.

Rite II

Praise to you, Lord Christ.

Gospel Tone II

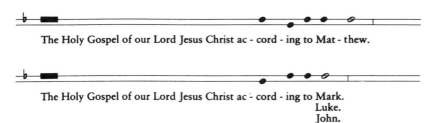

The Holy Gospel of our Lord Jesus Christ ac - cord - ing to Mat - thew.

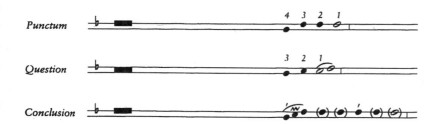

The Holy Gospel of our Lord Jesus Christ ac - cord - ing to Mark.
Luke.
John.

Punctum

Question

Conclusion

This tone, *of late 16th century origin, has no metrum, but only a punctum, in which the voice is dropped a minor third on the fourth syllable from the end of each sentence.*

Questions are sung as in Gospel Tone I.

The three-note group in the conclusion is sung to the next to the last accented syllable in the final sentence.

The phrase "The Gospel of the Lord" after the Gospel, and its response, are sung as at Gospel Tone I.

Prayers of the People

Form I, Tone A

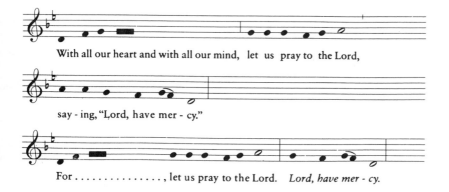

With all our heart and with all our mind, let us pray to the Lord,

say - ing, "Lord, have mer - cy."

For . . . . , let us pray to the Lord.   *Lord, have mer - cy.*

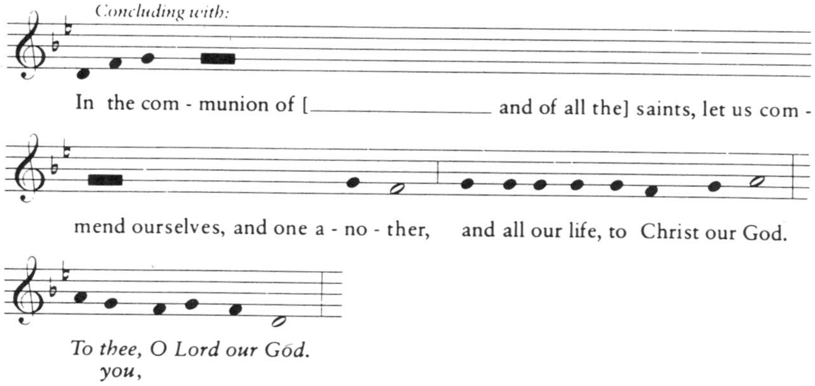
Concluding with:
In the com - munion of [______________ and of all the] saints, let us com -
mend ourselves, and one a - no - ther, and all our life, to Christ our God.
To thee, O Lord our God.
you,

Form I, Tone B (S106)

CD I TRACK 50

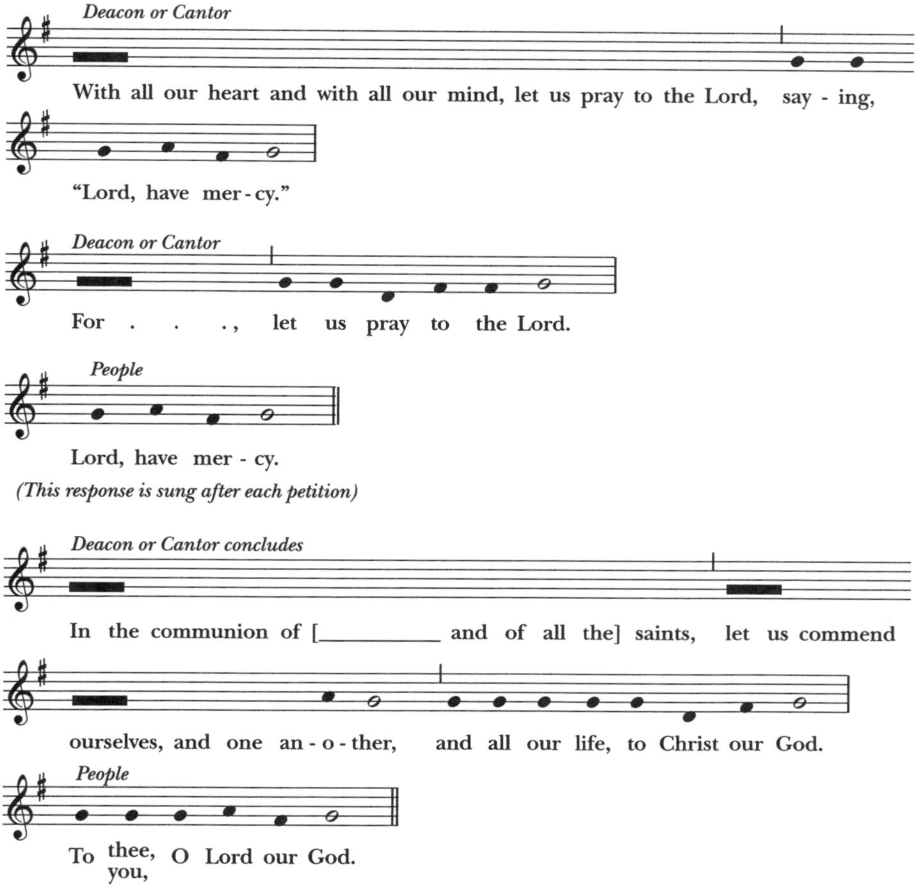
Deacon or Cantor
With all our heart and with all our mind, let us pray to the Lord, say - ing,
"Lord, have mer - cy."
Deacon or Cantor
For . . ., let us pray to the Lord.
People
Lord, have mer - cy.
(This response is sung after each petition)
Deacon or Cantor concludes
In the communion of [__________ and of all the] saints, let us commend
ourselves, and one an - o - ther, and all our life, to Christ our God.
People
To thee, O Lord our God.
you,

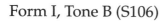

Deacon or leader

I ask your prayers for God's people through-out the world; for our Bishop(s)＿ ;

for this gathering; and for all minis - ters and peo - ple. Pray for the Church.

Silence

I ask your prayers for peace; for goodwill a - mong na - tions;

and for the well-being of all peo - ple. Pray for jus - tice and peace.

Silence

I ask your prayers for the poor, the sick, the hungry, the oppressed,

and those in pris - on. Pray for those in an - y need or trou - ble.

Silence

I ask your prayers for all who seek God, or a deeper know - ledge of him.

Pray that they may find and be found by him.

Silence

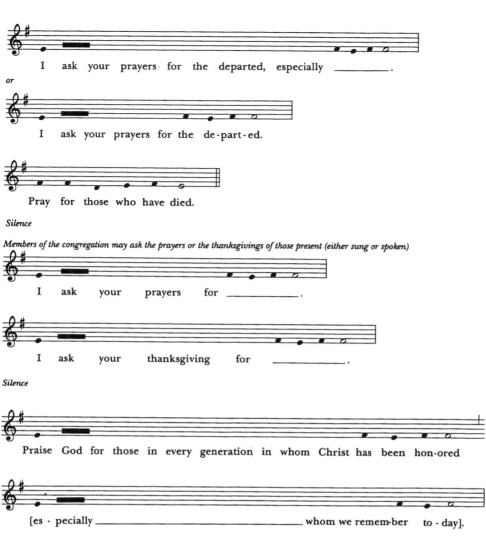

I ask your prayers · for the departed, especially _____.

or

I ask your prayers for the de-part-ed.

Pray for those who have died.

Silence

Members of the congregation may ask the prayers or the thanksgivings of those present (either sung or spoken)

I ask your prayers for _____.

I ask your thanksgiving for _____.

Silence

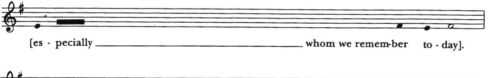

Praise God for those in every generation in whom Christ has been hon·ored

[es · pecially _____ whom we remem·ber to · day].

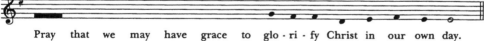

Pray that we may have grace to glo · ri · fy Christ in our own day.

Silence

The celebrant adds a concluding Collect which may be monotoned or sung to Collect Tone I or II, S 447 or S 448.

Setting: Adapt. David Hurd (b. 1950)

© 1982, David Hurd. Used by permission.

Form III (S107)

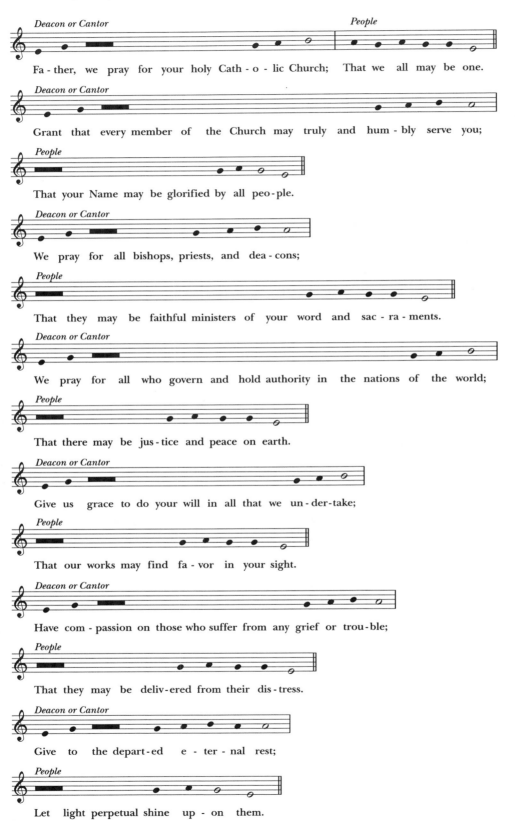

Deacon or Cantor / *People*

Fa - ther, we pray for your holy Cath - o - lic Church; That we all may be one.

Deacon or Cantor

Grant that every member of the Church may truly and hum - bly serve you;

People

That your Name may be glorified by all peo - ple.

Deacon or Cantor

We pray for all bishops, priests, and dea - cons;

People

That they may be faithful ministers of your word and sac - ra - ments.

Deacon or Cantor

We pray for all who govern and hold authority in the nations of the world;

People

That there may be jus - tice and peace on earth.

Deacon or Cantor

Give us grace to do your will in all that we un - der - take;

People

That our works may find fa - vor in your sight.

Deacon or Cantor

Have com - passion on those who suffer from any grief or trou - ble;

People

That they may be deliv - ered from their dis - tress.

Deacon or Cantor

Give to the depart - ed e - ter - nal rest;

People

Let light perpetual shine up - on them.

Deacon or Cantor

We praise you for your saints who have entered in-to joy;

People

May we also come to share in your hea-ven-ly king-dom.

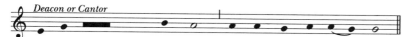

Deacon or Cantor

Let us pray for our own needs and the needs of o - thers.

Silence

The People may add their own petitions.

The Celebrant adds a concluding Collect which may be sung in monotone.

Setting: Anaphoral chant; adapt. Bruce E. Ford (b. 1947)

Form IV (S108)

CD II   TRACK 1

Deacon or Cantor

Let us pray for the Church and for the world.

Grant, Almighty God, that all who confess your Name may be united in your truth, live

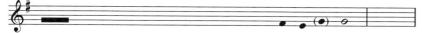

together in your love, and reveal your glory / in the word. *Silence*

Deacon or Cantor   *People (unison or harmony)*

Lord, in your mer-cy   Hear our prayer.

Form V, Tone A (S109)

CD II   TRACK 2

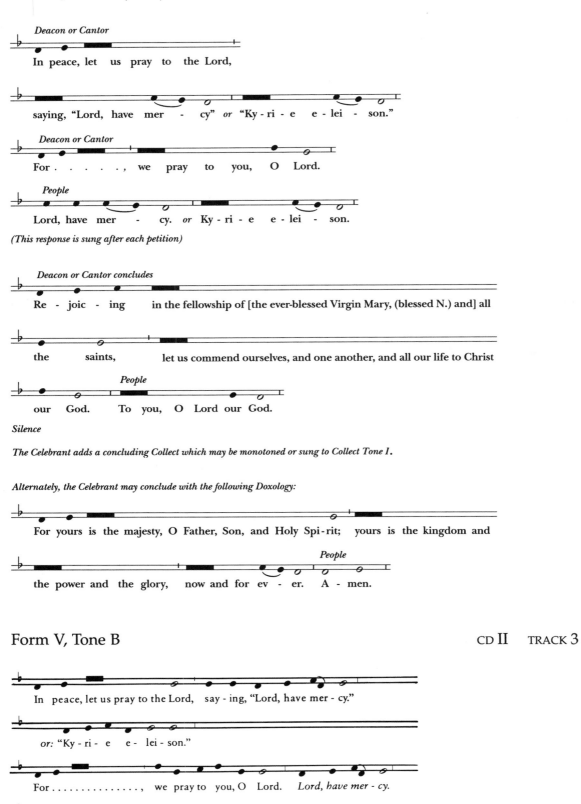

Deacon or Cantor

In peace, let us pray to the Lord,

saying, "Lord, have mer - cy" *or* "Ky - ri - e e - lei - son."

Deacon or Cantor

For . . . . . , we pray to you, O Lord.

People

Lord, have mer - cy. *or* Ky - ri - e e - lei - son.

(This response is sung after each petition)

Deacon or Cantor concludes

Re - joic - ing in the fellowship of [the ever-blessed Virgin Mary, (blessed N.) and] all

the saints, let us commend ourselves, and one another, and all our life to Christ

People

our God. To you, O Lord our God.

Silence

The Celebrant adds a concluding Collect which may be monotoned or sung to Collect Tone 1.

Alternately, the Celebrant may conclude with the following Doxology:

For yours is the majesty, O Father, Son, and Holy Spi - rit; yours is the kingdom and

People

the power and the glory, now and for ev - er. A - men.

Form V, Tone B

CD II   TRACK 3

In peace, let us pray to the Lord, say - ing, "Lord, have mer - cy."

or: "Ky - ri - e e - lei - son."

For . . . . , we pray to you, O Lord. *Lord, have mer - cy.*

or: Ky - ri - e e - lei - son.

Concluding with:

Re - joic - ing in the fellowship of [the ever-blessed Virgin Mary, *(blessed N.)* and] all

the saints, let us commend ourselves, and one another, and all our life to Christ

our God. *To you, O Lord our God.*

For yours is the majesty, O Father, Son and Holy Spi - rit; yours is the king -

dom and the power and the glo - ry, now and for ev - er. A - *men.*

Form VI (S363)

CD **II** TRACK 4

Leader

In peace, we pray to you, Lord God.   *Silence*

Leader

For all people in their daily life and work;

People

For our families, friends, and neighbors, and for those who are a - lone.

Leader

For this community, the nation, and the world;

People

For all who work for justice, freedom, and peace.

Leader

For the just and proper use of your crea - tion;

People

For the victims of hunger, fear, injustice, and oppres - sion.

Leader

For all who are in danger, sorrow, or any kind of trou - ble;

People

For those who minister to the sick, the friendless, and the need - y.

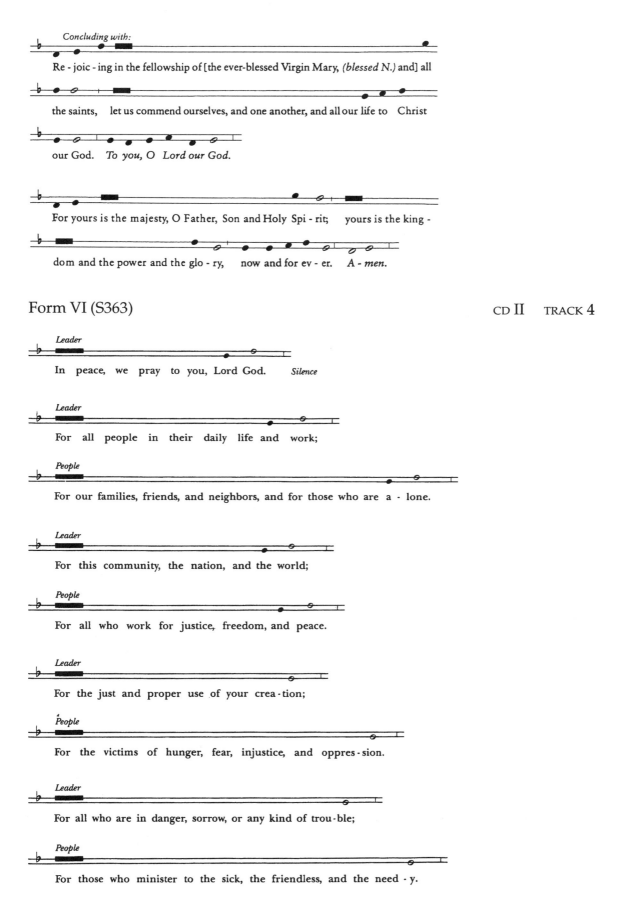

Leader

For the peace and unity of the Church of God;

People

For all who proclaim the Gospel, and all who seek the Truth.

Leader

For [N. our Presiding Bishop, and N.(N.) our Bishop(s); and for]

all bishops and other min - is - ters;

People

For all who serve God in his Church.

Leader

For the special needs and concerns of this congregation. *Silence*

The People may add their own petitions

Leader

Hear us Lord;

People

For your mer - cy is great.

Leader

We thank you, Lord, for all the blessings of this life. *Silence*

The People may add their own thanksgivings

Leader

We will exalt you, O God our King;

People

And praise your Name for ever and ev - er.

Leader

We pray for all who have died, that they may have a place in your

eternal king - dom. *Silence*

The People may add their own petitions

Leader

Lord, let your loving-kindness be upon them;

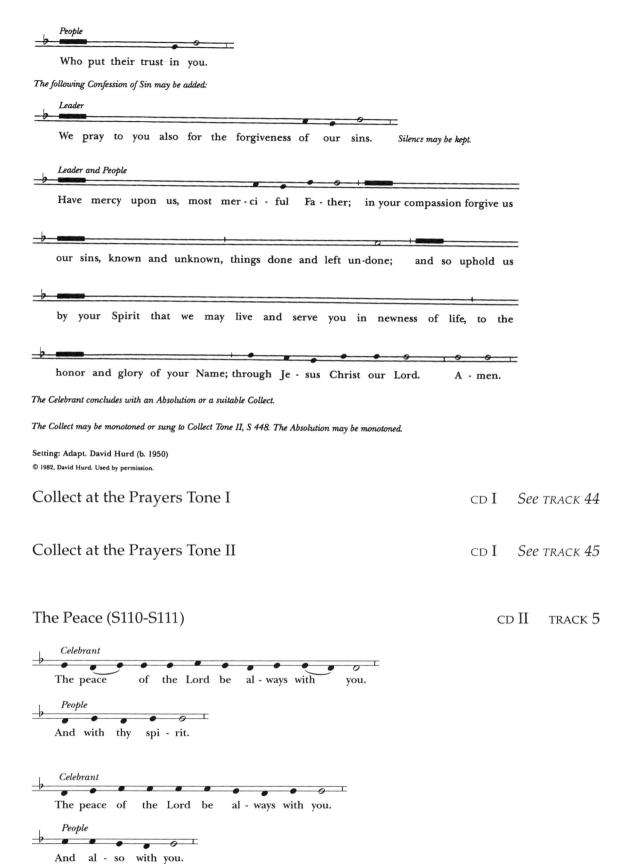

People

Who put their trust in you.

The following Confession of Sin may be added:

Leader

We pray to you also for the forgiveness of our sins.   *Silence may be kept.*

Leader and People

Have mercy upon us, most mer-ci-ful Fa-ther; in your compassion forgive us

our sins, known and unknown, things done and left un-done;   and so uphold us

by your Spirit that we may live and serve you in newness of life, to the

honor and glory of your Name; through Je-sus Christ our Lord.   A-men.

The Celebrant concludes with an Absolution or a suitable Collect.

The Collect may be monotoned or sung to Collect Tone II, S 448. The Absolution may be monotoned.

Setting: Adapt. David Hurd (b. 1950)

© 1982, David Hurd. Used by permission.

Collect at the Prayers Tone I

CD I   *See TRACK 44*

Collect at the Prayers Tone II

CD I   *See TRACK 45*

The Peace (S110-S111)

CD II   TRACK 5

Celebrant

The peace   of the Lord be al-ways with   you.

People

And with thy spi-rit.

Celebrant

The peace of the Lord be al-ways with you.

People

And al-so with you.

Setting: Ambrosian Chant; adapt. Mason Martens (b. 1933)

The Great Thanksgiving

Dialogue (S112)

CD II   TRACK 6

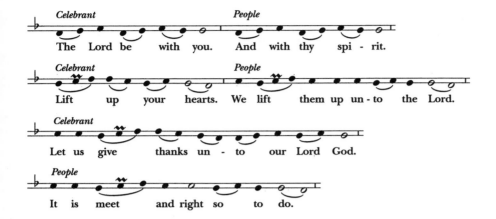

Celebrant: The Lord be with you.
People: And with thy spi-rit.

Celebrant: Lift up your hearts.
People: We lift them up un-to the Lord.

Celebrant: Let us give thanks un-to our Lord God.

People: It is meet and right so to do.

Prefaces Solemn Tone Rite I

The Lord's Day 1 (Of God the Father)

CD II   TRACK 7

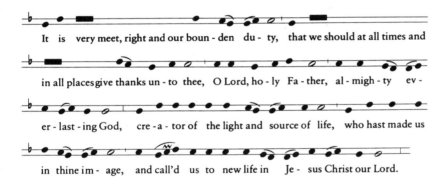

It is very meet, right and our boun-den du-ty, that we should at all times and in all places give thanks un-to thee, O Lord, ho-ly Fa-ther, al-migh-ty ev-er-last-ing God, cre-a-tor of the light and source of life, who hast made us in thine im-age, and call'd us to new life in Je-sus Christ our Lord.

The Lord's Day 2 (Of God the Son)

CD II   TRACK 8

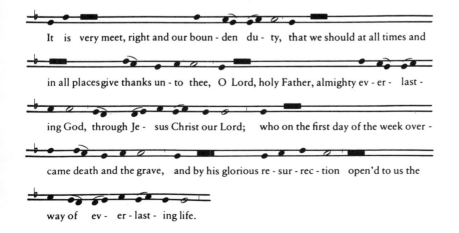

It is very meet, right and our boun-den du-ty, that we should at all times and in all places give thanks un-to thee, O Lord, holy Father, almighty ev-er-last-ing God, through Je-sus Christ our Lord; who on the first day of the week over-came death and the grave, and by his glorious re-sur-rec-tion open'd to us the way of ev-er-last-ing life.

The Lord's Day 3 (Of God the Holy Spirit)

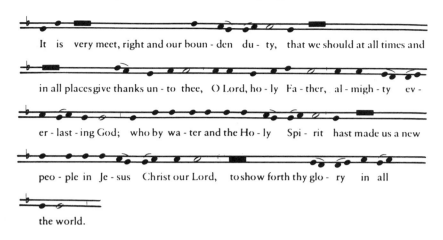

It is very meet, right and our boun - den du - ty, that we should at all times and in all places give thanks un - to thee, O Lord, ho - ly Fa - ther, al - migh - ty ev - er - last - ing God; who by wa - ter and the Ho - ly Spi - rit hast made us a new peo - ple in Je - sus Christ our Lord, to show forth thy glo - ry in all the world.

Weekdays after Pentecost

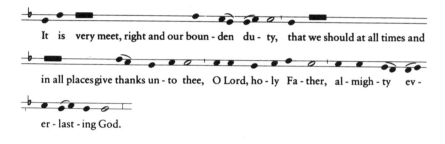

It is very meet, right and our boun - den du - ty, that we should at all times and in all places give thanks un - to thee, O Lord, ho - ly Fa - ther, al - migh - ty ev - er - last - ing God.

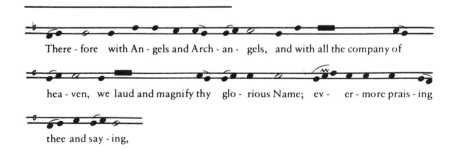

There - fore with An - gels and Arch - an - gels, and with all the company of hea - ven, we laud and magnify thy glo - rious Name; ev - er - more prais - ing thee and say - ing,

Advent

It is very meet, right and our boun - den du - ty, that we should at all times and in all places give thanks un - to thee, O Lord, ho - ly Fa - ther, al - migh - ty ev - er - last - ing God; be - cause thou didst send thy be - lov - ed Son to re - deem us from sin and death, and to make us heirs in him of ev - er - last - ing life; that when he shall come again in power and great tri - umph to judge the world, we may with - out shame or fear re - joice to be - hold his ap - pear - ing.

Incarnation

It is very meet, right and our boun - den du - ty, that we should at all times and in all places give thanks un - to thee, O Lord, ho - ly Fa - ther, al - migh - ty ev - er - last - ing God; be - cause thou didst give Jesus Christ thine only Son to be born for us; who, by the mighty power of the Ho - ly Ghost, was made ve - ry Man of the substance of the Vir - gin Ma - ry his mo - ther; that we might be deliver'd from the bon - dage of sin, and re - ceive pow'r to be - come thy child - ren.

Epiphany

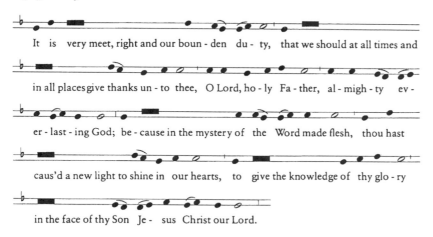

It is very meet, right and our boun-den du-ty, that we should at all times and in all places give thanks un-to thee, O Lord, ho-ly Fa-ther, al-migh-ty ev-er-last-ing God; be-cause in the mystery of the Word made flesh, thou hast caus'd a new light to shine in our hearts, to give the knowledge of thy glo-ry in the face of thy Son Je-sus Christ our Lord.

Lent (1)

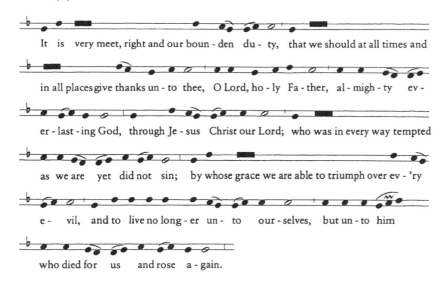

It is very meet, right and our boun-den du-ty, that we should at all times and in all places give thanks un-to thee, O Lord, ho-ly Fa-ther, al-migh-ty ev-er-last-ing God, through Je-sus Christ our Lord; who was in every way tempted as we are yet did not sin; by whose grace we are able to triumph over ev-'ry e-vil, and to live no long-er un-to our-selves, but un-to him who died for us and rose a-gain.

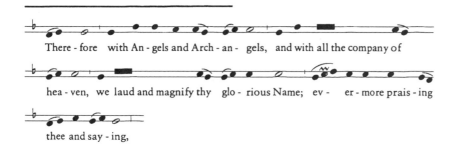

There-fore with An-gels and Arch-an-gels, and with all the company of hea-ven, we laud and magnify thy glo-rious Name; ev-er-more prais-ing thee and say-ing,

Lent (2)

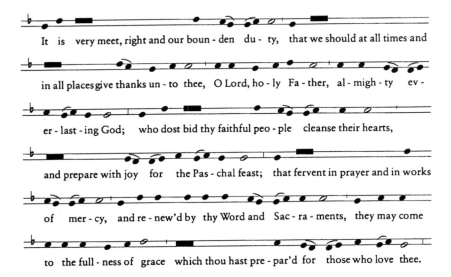

It is very meet, right and our boun - den du - ty, that we should at all times and in all places give thanks un - to thee, O Lord, ho - ly Fa - ther, al - migh - ty ev - er - last - ing God; who dost bid thy faithful peo - ple cleanse their hearts, and prepare with joy for the Pas - chal feast; that fervent in prayer and in works of mer - cy, and re - new'd by thy Word and Sac - ra - ments, they may come to the full - ness of grace which thou hast pre - par'd for those who love thee.

Holy Week

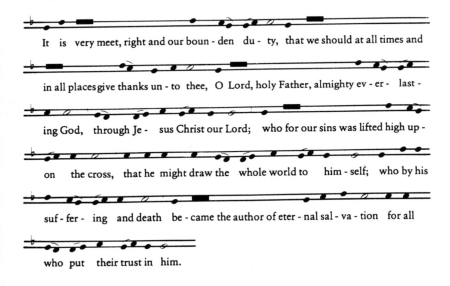

It is very meet, right and our boun - den du - ty, that we should at all times and in all places give thanks un - to thee, O Lord, holy Father, almighty ev - er - last - ing God, through Je - sus Christ our Lord; who for our sins was lifted high up - on the cross, that he might draw the whole world to him - self; who by his suf - fer - ing and death be - came the author of eter - nal sal - va - tion for all who put their trust in him.

Easter

It is very meet, right and our boun - den du - ty, that we should at all times and

in all places give thanks un - to thee, O Lord, ho - ly Fa - ther, al - migh - ty ev -

er - last - ing God; but chiefly are we bound to praise thee for the glo - rious re -

sur - rec - tion of thy Son Je - sus Christ our Lord; for he is the ve - ry

Pas - chal Lamb, who was sac - ri - fic'd for us, and hath ta - ken a - way the

sin of the world; who by his death hath de - stroy'd death, and by his ris - ing

to life a - gain hath won for us ev - er - last - ing life.

Ascension

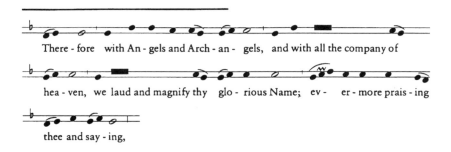

It is very meet, right and our boun - den du - ty, that we should at all times and

in all places give thanks un - to thee, O Lord, holy Father, almighty ev - er - last -

ing God, through thy dear - ly be - lov - ed Son Je - sus Christ our Lord; who

after his glorious re - sur - rec - tion man - i - fest - ly ap - pear'd to his dis -

ci - ples; and in their sight ascended in - to hea - ven, to pre - pare a place

for us; that where he is, there we might al - so be, and reign with him

in glo - ry.

There - fore with An - gels and Arch - an - gels, and with all the company of

hea - ven, we laud and magnify thy glo - rious Name; ev - er - more prais - ing

thee and say - ing,

Pentecost

It is very meet, right and our boun - den du - ty, that we should at all times and

in all places give thanks un - to thee, O Lord, holy Father, almighty ev - er - last -

ing God, through Je - sus Christ our Lord; ac - cord - ing to whose true pro - mise

the Holy Ghost came down [on this day] from hea - ven, light - ing up - on the dis -

ci - ples, to teach them and to lead them in - to all truth; u - niting peoples

of many tongues in the con - fes - sion of one faith, and giving to thy Church the

power to serve thee as a roy - al priest - hood, and to preach the Gos - pel to

all na - tions.

Trinity Sunday

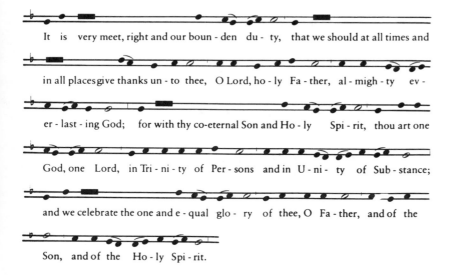

It is very meet, right and our boun - den du - ty, that we should at all times and

in all places give thanks un - to thee, O Lord, ho - ly Fa - ther, al - migh - ty ev -

er - last - ing God; for with thy co-eternal Son and Ho - ly Spi - rit, thou art one

God, one Lord, in Tri - ni - ty of Per - sons and in U - ni - ty of Sub - stance;

and we celebrate the one and e - qual glo - ry of thee, O Fa - ther, and of the

Son, and of the Ho - ly Spi - rit.

All Saints

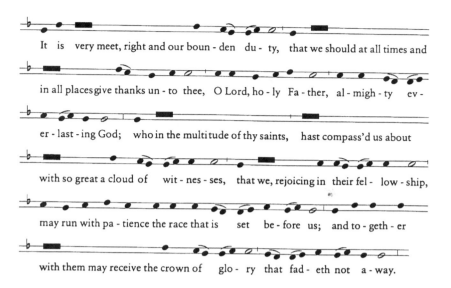

It is very meet, right and our boun-den du-ty, that we should at all times and in all places give thanks un-to thee, O Lord, ho-ly Fa-ther, al-migh-ty ev-er-last-ing God; who in the multitude of thy saints, hast compass'd us about with so great a cloud of wit-nes-ses, that we, rejoicing in their fel-low-ship, may run with pa-tience the race that is set be-fore us; and to-geth-er with them may receive the crown of glo-ry that fad-eth not a-way.

A Saint (1)

It is very meet, right and our boun-den du-ty, that we should at all times and in all places give thanks un-to thee, O Lord, holy Father, almighty ev-er-last-ing God, for the won-der-ful grace and vir-tue de-clar'd in all thy saints, who have been the cho-sen ves-sels of thy grace, and the lights of the world in their ge-ne-ra-tions.

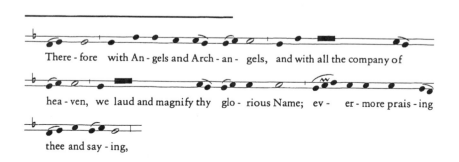

There-fore with An-gels and Arch-an-gels, and with all the company of hea-ven, we laud and magnify thy glo-rious Name; ev-er-more prais-ing thee and say-ing,

A Saint (2)

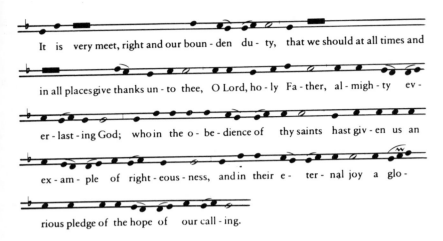

It is very meet, right and our boun - den du - ty, that we should at all times and in all places give thanks un - to thee, O Lord, ho - ly Fa - ther, al - migh - ty ev - er - last - ing God; who in the o - be - dience of thy saints hast giv - en us an ex - am - ple of right - eous - ness, and in their e - ter - nal joy a glo - rious pledge of the hope of our call - ing.

A Saint (3)

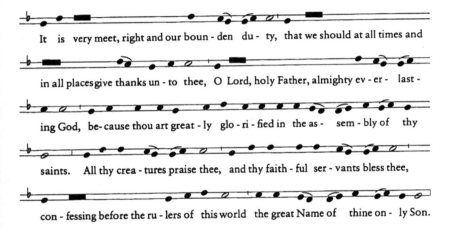

It is very meet, right and our boun - den du - ty, that we should at all times and in all places give thanks un - to thee, O Lord, holy Father, almighty ev - er - last - ing God, be - cause thou art great - ly glo - ri - fied in the as - sem - bly of thy saints. All thy crea - tures praise thee, and thy faith - ful ser - vants bless thee, con - fessing before the ru - lers of this world the great Name of thine on - ly Son.

Apostles and Ordinations

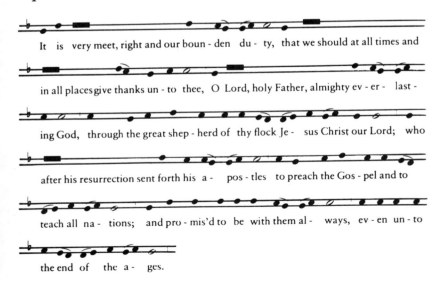

It is very meet, right and our boun - den du - ty, that we should at all times and in all places give thanks un - to thee, O Lord, holy Father, almighty ev - er - last - ing God, through the great shep - herd of thy flock Je - sus Christ our Lord; who after his resurrection sent forth his a - pos - tles to preach the Gos - pel and to teach all na - tions; and pro - mis'd to be with them al - ways, ev - en un - to the end of the a - ges.

Dedication of a Church

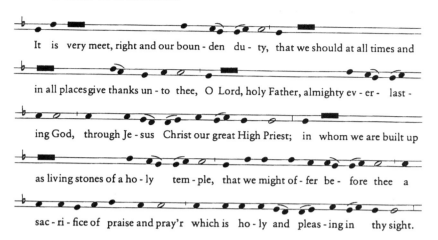

It is very meet, right and our boun-den du-ty, that we should at all times and in all places give thanks un-to thee, O Lord, holy Father, almighty ev-er-last-ing God, through Je-sus Christ our great High Priest; in whom we are built up as living stones of a ho-ly tem-ple, that we might of-fer be-fore thee a sac-ri-fice of praise and pray'r which is ho-ly and pleas-ing in thy sight.

Baptism

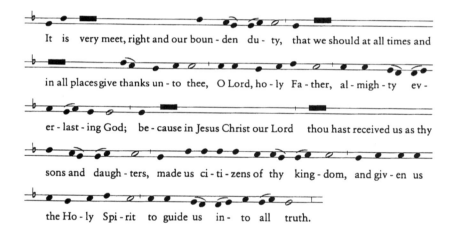

It is very meet, right and our boun-den du-ty, that we should at all times and in all places give thanks un-to thee, O Lord, ho-ly Fa-ther, al-migh-ty ev-er-last-ing God; be-cause in Jesus Christ our Lord thou hast received us as thy sons and daugh-ters, made us ci-ti-zens of thy king-dom, and giv-en us the Ho-ly Spi-rit to guide us in-to all truth.

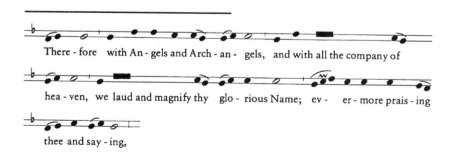

There-fore with An-gels and Arch-an-gels, and with all the company of hea-ven, we laud and magnify thy glo-rious Name; ev-er-more prais-ing thee and say-ing,

Marriage

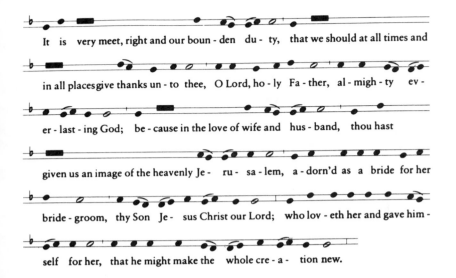

It is very meet, right and our boun - den du - ty, that we should at all times and in all places give thanks un - to thee, O Lord, ho - ly Fa - ther, al - migh - ty ev - er - last - ing God; be - cause in the love of wife and hus - band, thou hast given us an image of the heavenly Je - ru - sa - lem, a - dorn'd as a bride for her bride - groom, thy Son Je - sus Christ our Lord; who lov - eth her and gave him - self for her, that he might make the whole cre - a - tion new.

Commemoration of the Dead

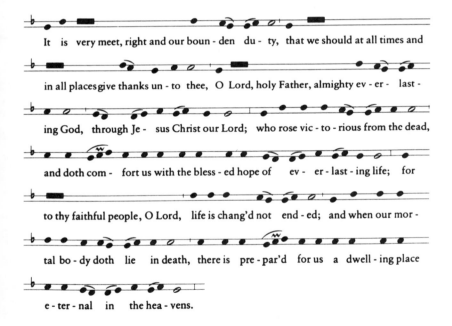

It is very meet, right and our boun - den du - ty, that we should at all times and in all places give thanks un - to thee, O Lord, holy Father, almighty ev - er - last - ing God, through Je - sus Christ our Lord; who rose vic - to - rious from the dead, and doth com - fort us with the bless - ed hope of ev - er - last - ing life; for to thy faithful people, O Lord, life is chang'd not end - ed; and when our mor - tal bo - dy doth lie in death, there is pre - par'd for us a dwell - ing place e - ter - nal in the hea - vens.

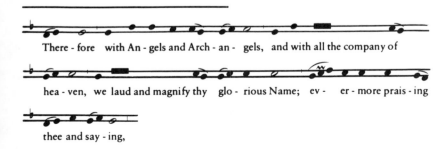

There - fore with An - gels and Arch - an - gels, and with all the company of hea - ven, we laud and magnify thy glo - rious Name; ev - er - more prais - ing thee and say - ing,

Prefaces Simple Tone Rite I

The Lord's Day 1 (Of God the Father)

CD II   TRACK 30

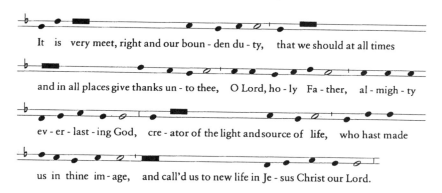

It is very meet, right and our boun-den du-ty, that we should at all times and in all places give thanks un-to thee, O Lord, ho-ly Fa-ther, al-migh-ty ev-er-last-ing God, cre-ator of the light and source of life, who hast made us in thine im-age, and call'd us to new life in Je-sus Christ our Lord.

The Lord's Day 2 (Of God the Son)

CD II   TRACK 31

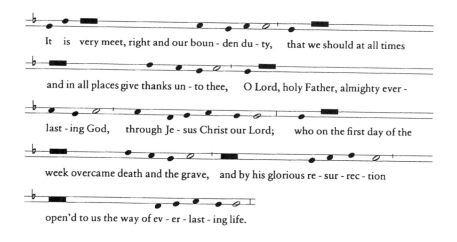

It is very meet, right and our boun-den du-ty, that we should at all times and in all places give thanks un-to thee, O Lord, holy Father, almighty ever-last-ing God, through Je-sus Christ our Lord; who on the first day of the week overcame death and the grave, and by his glorious re-sur-rec-tion open'd to us the way of ev-er-last-ing life.

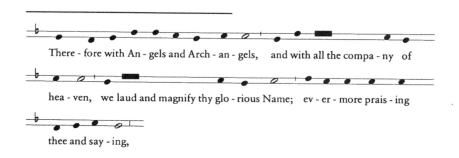

There-fore with An-gels and Arch-an-gels, and with all the compa-ny of hea-ven, we laud and magnify thy glo-rious Name; ev-er-more prais-ing thee and say-ing,

The Lord's Day 3 (Of God the Holy Spirit)

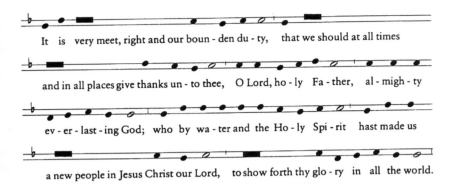

It is very meet, right and our boun-den du-ty, that we should at all times and in all places give thanks un-to thee, O Lord, ho-ly Fa-ther, al-migh-ty ev-er-last-ing God; who by wa-ter and the Ho-ly Spi-rit hast made us a new people in Jesus Christ our Lord, to show forth thy glo-ry in all the world.

Weekdays after Pentecost

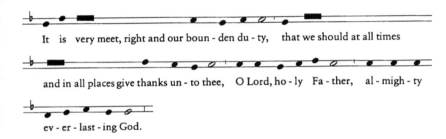

It is very meet, right and our boun-den du-ty, that we should at all times and in all places give thanks un-to thee, O Lord, ho-ly Fa-ther, al-migh-ty ev-er-last-ing God.

Advent

It is very meet, right and our boun-den du-ty, that we should at all times and in all places give thanks un-to thee, O Lord, ho-ly Fa-ther, al-migh-ty ev-er-last-ing God; be-cause thou didst send thy be-lov-ed Son to re-deem us from sin and death, and to make us heirs in him of ev-er-last-ing life; that when he shall come again in power and great triumph to judge the world, we may without shame or fear re-joice to be-hold his ap-pear-ing.

Incarnation

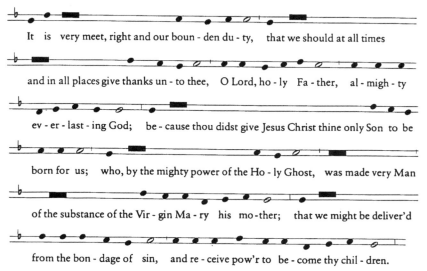

It is very meet, right and our boun - den du - ty, that we should at all times

and in all places give thanks un - to thee, O Lord, ho - ly Fa - ther, al - migh - ty

ev - er - last - ing God; be - cause thou didst give Jesus Christ thine only Son to be

born for us; who, by the mighty power of the Ho - ly Ghost, was made very Man

of the substance of the Vir - gin Ma - ry his mo - ther; that we might be deliver'd

from the bon - dage of sin, and re - ceive pow'r to be - come thy chil - dren.

Epiphany

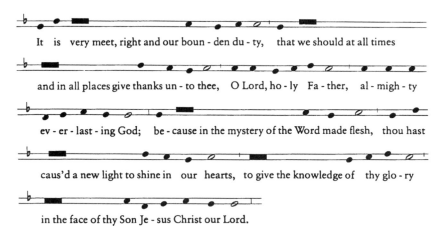

It is very meet, right and our boun - den du - ty, that we should at all times

and in all places give thanks un - to thee, O Lord, ho - ly Fa - ther, al - migh - ty

ev - er - last - ing God; be - cause in the mystery of the Word made flesh, thou hast

caus'd a new light to shine in our hearts, to give the knowledge of thy glo - ry

in the face of thy Son Je - sus Christ our Lord.

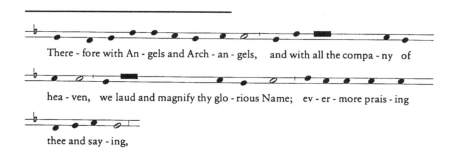

There - fore with An - gels and Arch - an - gels, and with all the compa - ny of

hea - ven, we laud and magnify thy glo - rious Name; ev - er - more prais - ing

thee and say - ing,

Lent (1)

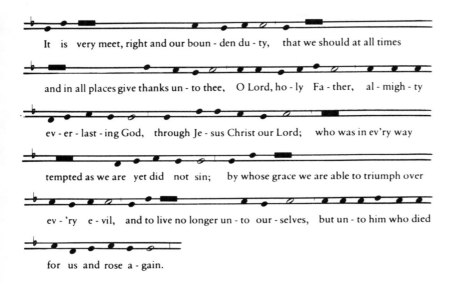

It is very meet, right and our boun-den du-ty, that we should at all times and in all places give thanks un-to thee, O Lord, ho-ly Fa-ther, al-migh-ty ev-er-last-ing God, through Je-sus Christ our Lord; who was in ev'ry way tempted as we are yet did not sin; by whose grace we are able to triumph over ev-'ry e-vil, and to live no longer un-to our-selves, but un-to him who died for us and rose a-gain.

Lent (2)

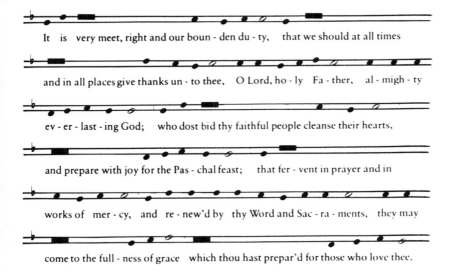

It is very meet, right and our boun-den du-ty, that we should at all times and in all places give thanks un-to thee, O Lord, ho-ly Fa-ther, al-migh-ty ev-er-last-ing God; who dost bid thy faithful people cleanse their hearts, and prepare with joy for the Pas-chal feast; that fer-vent in prayer and in works of mer-cy, and re-new'd by thy Word and Sac-ra-ments, they may come to the full-ness of grace which thou hast prepar'd for those who love thee.

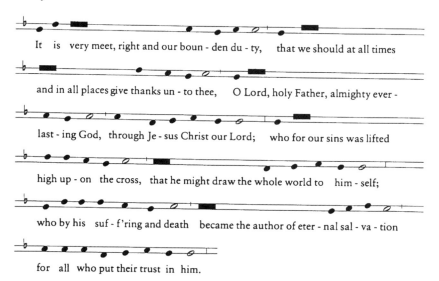

It is very meet, right and our boun - den du - ty, that we should at all times and in all places give thanks un - to thee, O Lord, holy Father, almighty ever - last - ing God, through Je - sus Christ our Lord; who for our sins was lifted high up - on the cross, that he might draw the whole world to him - self; who by his suf - f'ring and death became the author of eter - nal sal - va - tion for all who put their trust in him.

Easter

It is very meet, right and our boun - den du - ty, that we should at all times and in all places give thanks un - to thee, O Lord, ho - ly Fa - ther, al - migh - ty ev - er - last - ing God; but chief - ly are we bound to praise thee for the glo - rious re - sur - rec - tion of thy Son Je - sus Christ our Lord; for he is the very Paschal Lamb, who was sacri - fic'd for us, and hath taken away the sin of the world; who by his death hath de - stroy'd death, and by his ris - ing to life a - gain hath won for us ev - er - last - ing life.

There - fore with An - gels and Arch - an - gels, and with all the compa - ny of hea - ven, we laud and magnify thy glo - rious Name; ev - er - more prais - ing thee and say - ing,

Ascension

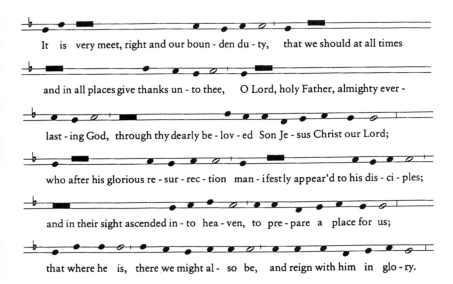

It is very meet, right and our boun-den du-ty, that we should at all times and in all places give thanks un-to thee, O Lord, holy Father, almighty ever-last-ing God, through thy dearly be-lov-ed Son Je-sus Christ our Lord; who after his glorious re-sur-rec-tion man-ifestly appear'd to his dis-ci-ples; and in their sight ascended in-to hea-ven, to pre-pare a place for us; that where he is, there we might al-so be, and reign with him in glo-ry.

Pentecost

It is very meet, right and our boun-den du-ty, that we should at all times and in all places give thanks un-to thee, O Lord, holy Father, almighty ever-last-ing God, through Je-sus Christ our Lord; ac-cord-ing to whose true pro-mise the Holy Ghost came down [on this day] from heaven, light-ing up-on the dis-ci-ples, to teach them and to lead them in-to all truth; u-niting peoples of many tongues in the confession of one faith, and giving to thy Church the power to serve thee as a roy-al priest-hood, and to preach the Gos-pel to all na-tions.

Trinity Sunday

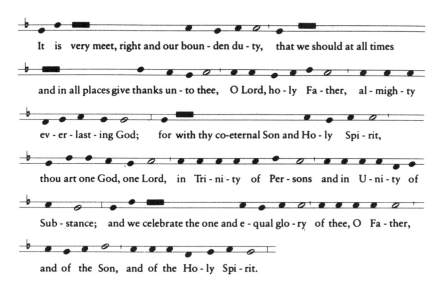

It is very meet, right and our boun - den du - ty, that we should at all times

and in all places give thanks un - to thee, O Lord, ho - ly Fa - ther, al - migh - ty

ev - er - last - ing God; for with thy co-eternal Son and Ho - ly Spi - rit,

thou art one God, one Lord, in Tri - ni - ty of Per - sons and in U - ni - ty of

Sub - stance; and we celebrate the one and e - qual glo - ry of thee, O Fa - ther,

and of the Son, and of the Ho - ly Spi - rit.

All Saints

It is very meet, right and our boun - den du - ty, that we should at all times

and in all places give thanks un - to thee, O Lord, ho - ly Fa - ther, al - migh - ty

ev - er - last - ing God; who in the multitude of thy saints, hast compass'd us about

with so great a cloud of wit - nes - ses, that we, re - joi - cing in their fel - low - ship,

may run with pa - tience the race that is set be - fore us; and, to - gether with them,

may receive the crown of glo - ry that fa - deth not a - way.

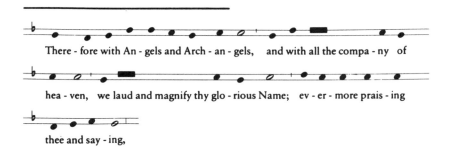

There - fore with An - gels and Arch - an - gels, and with all the compa - ny of

hea - ven, we laud and magnify thy glo - rious Name; ev - er - more prais - ing

thee and say - ing,

A Saint (1)

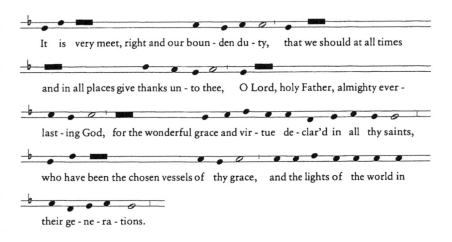

It is very meet, right and our boun - den du - ty, that we should at all times and in all places give thanks un - to thee, O Lord, holy Father, almighty ever - last - ing God, for the wonderful grace and vir - tue de - clar'd in all thy saints, who have been the chosen vessels of thy grace, and the lights of the world in their ge - ne - ra - tions.

A Saint (2)

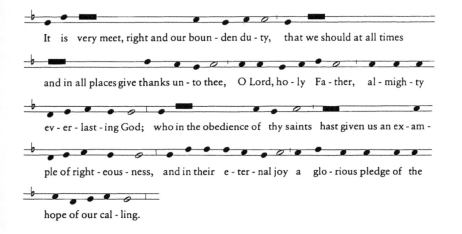

It is very meet, right and our boun - den du - ty, that we should at all times and in all places give thanks un - to thee, O Lord, ho - ly Fa - ther, al - migh - ty ev - er - last - ing God; who in the obedience of thy saints hast given us an ex - am - ple of right - eous - ness, and in their e - ter - nal joy a glo - rious pledge of the hope of our cal - ling.

A Saint (3)

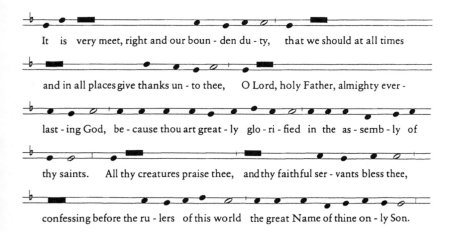

It is very meet, right and our boun - den du - ty, that we should at all times and in all places give thanks un - to thee, O Lord, holy Father, almighty ever - last - ing God, be - cause thou art great - ly glo - ri - fied in the as - semb - ly of thy saints. All thy creatures praise thee, and thy faithful ser - vants bless thee, confessing before the ru - lers of this world the great Name of thine on - ly Son.

Apostles and Ordinations

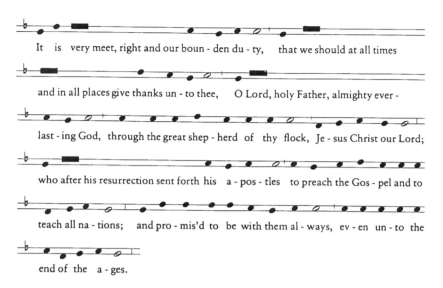

It is very meet, right and our boun - den du - ty, that we should at all times and in all places give thanks un - to thee, O Lord, holy Father, almighty ever - last - ing God, through the great shep - herd of thy flock, Je - sus Christ our Lord; who after his resurrection sent forth his a - pos - tles to preach the Gos - pel and to teach all na - tions; and pro - mis'd to be with them al - ways, ev - en un - to the end of the a - ges.

Dedication of a Church

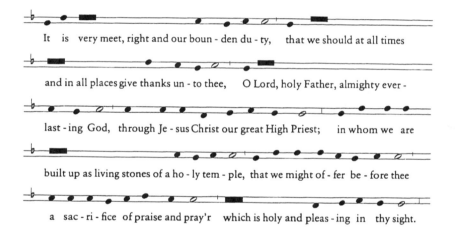

It is very meet, right and our boun - den du - ty, that we should at all times and in all places give thanks un - to thee, O Lord, holy Father, almighty ever - last - ing God, through Je - sus Christ our great High Priest; in whom we are built up as living stones of a ho - ly tem - ple, that we might of - fer be - fore thee a sac - ri - fice of praise and pray'r which is holy and pleas - ing in thy sight.

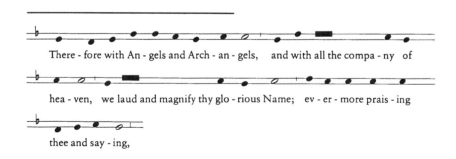

There - fore with An - gels and Arch - an - gels, and with all the compa - ny of hea - ven, we laud and magnify thy glo - rious Name; ev - er - more prais - ing thee and say - ing,

Baptism

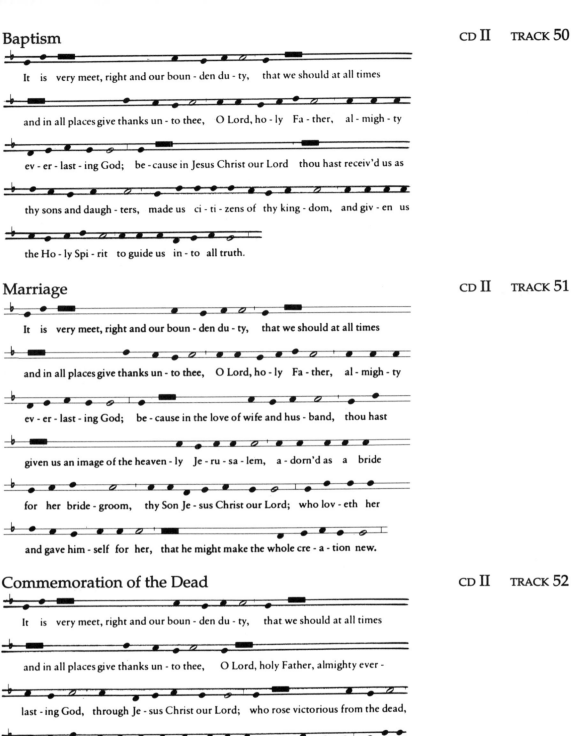

It is very meet, right and our boun-den du-ty, that we should at all times and in all places give thanks un-to thee, O Lord, ho-ly Fa-ther, al-migh-ty ev-er-last-ing God; be-cause in Jesus Christ our Lord thou hast receiv'd us as thy sons and daugh-ters, made us ci-ti-zens of thy king-dom, and giv-en us the Ho-ly Spi-rit to guide us in-to all truth.

Marriage

It is very meet, right and our boun-den du-ty, that we should at all times and in all places give thanks un-to thee, O Lord, ho-ly Fa-ther, al-migh-ty ev-er-last-ing God; be-cause in the love of wife and hus-band, thou hast given us an image of the heaven-ly Je-ru-sa-lem, a-dorn'd as a bride for her bride-groom, thy Son Je-sus Christ our Lord; who lov-eth her and gave him-self for her, that he might make the whole cre-a-tion new.

Commemoration of the Dead

It is very meet, right and our boun-den du-ty, that we should at all times and in all places give thanks un-to thee, O Lord, holy Father, almighty ever-last-ing God, through Je-sus Christ our Lord; who rose victorious from the dead, and doth com-fort us with the bless-ed hope of ev-er-last-ing life; for to thy faithful people, O Lord, life is chang'd, not end-ed; and when our mortal body doth lie in death, there is pre-par'd for us a dwell-ing place e-ter-nal in the hea-vens.

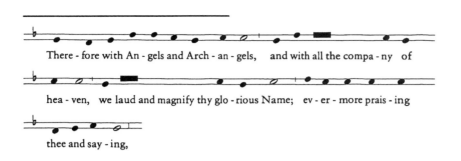

There - fore with An - gels and Arch - an - gels, and with all the compa - ny of

hea - ven, we laud and magnify thy glo - rious Name; ev - er - more prais - ing

thee and say - ing,

Conclusion of the Eucharistic Prayer Rite I

Solemn Tone, Prayer I

CD II   TRACK 53

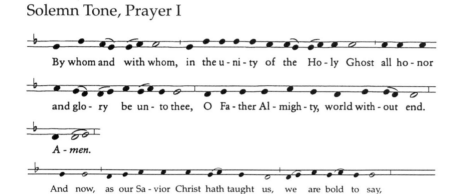

By whom and with whom, in the u - ni - ty of the Ho - ly Ghost all ho - nor

and glo - ry be un - to thee, O Fa - ther Al - migh - ty, world with - out end.

A - men.

And now, as our Sa - vior Christ hath taught us, we are bold to say,

Simple Tone, Prayer I

CD II   TRACK 54

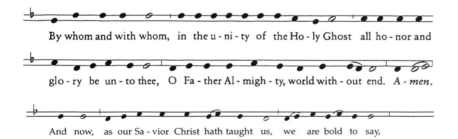

By whom and with whom, in the u - ni - ty of the Ho - ly Ghost all ho - nor and

glo - ry be un - to thee, O Fa - ther Al - migh - ty, world with - out end. A - men.

And now, as our Sa - vior Christ hath taught us, we are bold to say,

Solemn Tone, Prayer II

CD II   TRACK 55

By whom and with whom and in whom, in the u - ni - ty of the Ho - ly

Ghost all ho - nor and glo - ry be un - to thee, O Fa - ther Al - migh - ty,

world with - out end. A - men.

And now, as our Sa - vior Christ hath taught us, we are bold to say,

Simple Tone, Prayer II

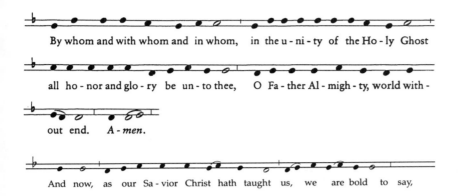

By whom and with whom and in whom, in the u - ni - ty of the Ho - ly Ghost all ho - nor and glo - ry be un - to thee, O Fa - ther Al - migh - ty, world with - out end. *A - men.*

And now, as our Sa - vior Christ hath taught us, we are bold to say,

Christ our Passover and Christ our Passover with Alleluias (S152-3)

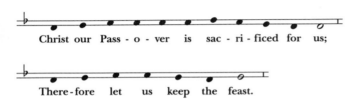

Christ our Pass - o - ver is sac - ri - ficed for us;

There - fore let us keep the feast.

This setting may be sung full by all, or by the choir, or as a versicle and response.

Setting: Ambrosian chant; adapt. Mason Martens (1933-1991)

This setting is not used in Lent.

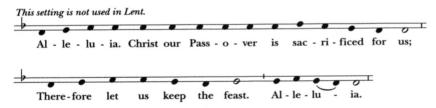

Al - le - lu - ia. Christ our Pass - o - ver is sac - ri - ficed for us;

There - fore let us keep the feast. Al - le - lu - ia.

This setting may be sung full by all, or by the choir, or as a versicle and response.

Setting: Ambrosian chant; adapt. Mason Martens (1933-1991)

Invitation to Communion

Tone I

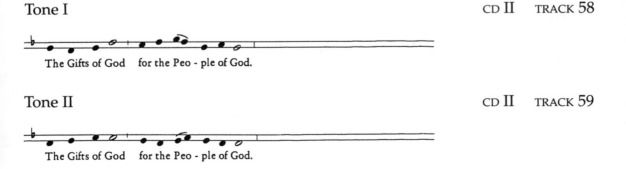

The Gifts of God for the Peo - ple of God.

Tone II

The Gifts of God for the Peo - ple of God.

Blessing

Shorter Form

CD II   TRACK 60

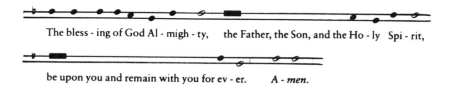

The bless - ing of God Al - migh - ty,   the Father, the Son, and the Ho - ly Spi - rit,

be upon you and remain with you for ev - er.   A - men.

Longer Form

CD II   TRACK 61

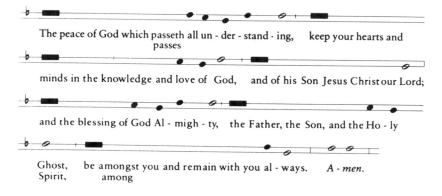

The peace of God which passeth all un - der - stand - ing,   keep your hearts and
                          passes

minds in the knowledge and love of God,   and of his Son Jesus Christ our Lord;

and the blessing of God Al - migh - ty,   the Father, the Son, and the Ho - ly

Ghost,   be amongst you and remain with you al - ways.   A - men.
Spirit,   among

Pontifical Blessing (S173)

CD II   TRACK 62

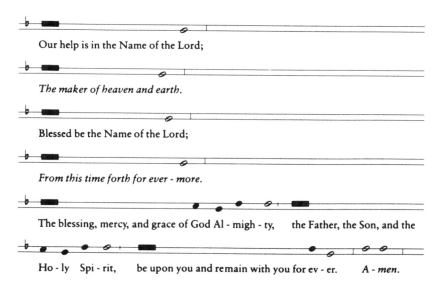

Our help is in the Name of the Lord;

The maker of heaven and earth.

Blessed be the Name of the Lord;

From this time forth for ever - more.

The blessing, mercy, and grace of God Al - migh - ty,   the Father, the Son, and the

Ho - ly Spi - rit,   be upon you and remain with you for ev - er.   A - men.

Blessing at the Ordination of a Priest

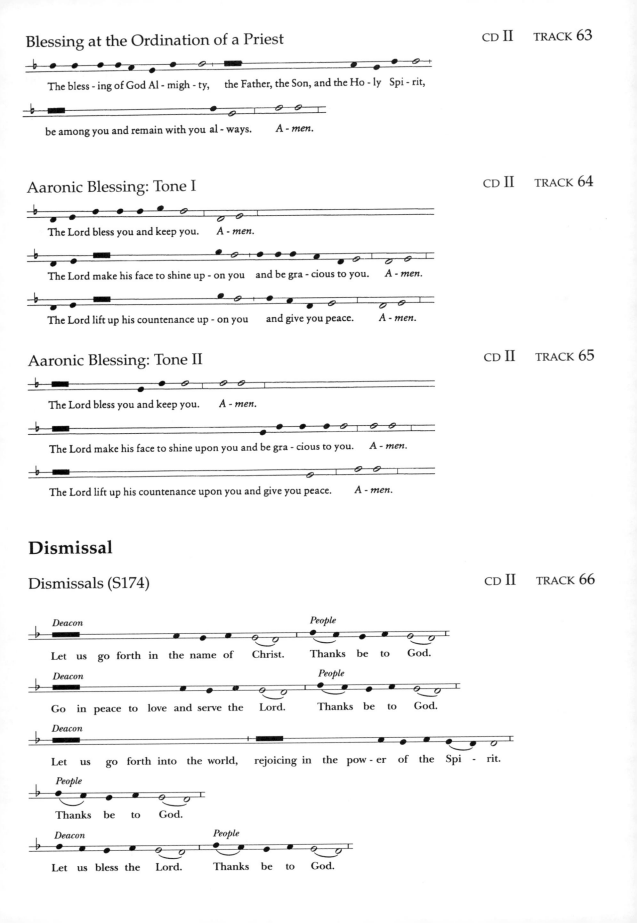

The bless - ing of God Al - migh - ty,   the Father, the Son, and the Ho - ly Spi - rit,

be among you and remain with you al - ways.   A - *men.*

Aaronic Blessing: Tone I

The Lord bless you and keep you.   A - *men.*

The Lord make his face to shine up - on you and be gra - cious to you.   A - *men.*

The Lord lift up his countenance up - on you   and give you peace.   A - *men.*

Aaronic Blessing: Tone II

The Lord bless you and keep you.   A - *men.*

The Lord make his face to shine upon you and be gra - cious to you.   A - *men.*

The Lord lift up his countenance upon you and give you peace.   A - *men.*

Dismissal

Dismissals (S174)

Deacon   *People*

Let us go forth in the name of Christ.   Thanks be to God.

Deacon   *People*

Go in peace to love and serve the Lord.   Thanks be to God.

Deacon

Let us go forth into the world, rejoicing in the pow - er of the Spi - rit.

People

Thanks be to God.

Deacon   *People*

Let us bless the Lord.   Thanks be to God.

Let us go forth in the name of Christ, al - le - lu - ia,

al - le - lu - ia.

Thanks be to God, al - le - lu - ia, al - le - lu - ia.

or

Go in peace to love and serve the Lord, al - le - lu - ia,

al - le - lu - ia.

Thanks be to God, al - le - lu - ia, al - le - lu - ia.

Let us go forth into the world, rejoicing in the power of the Spi - rit,

al - le - lu - ia, al - le - lu - ia.

Thanks be to God, al - le - lu - ia, al - le - lu - ia.

or the following

Let us bless the Lord, al - le - lu - ia, al - le - lu - ia.

Thanks be to God, al - le - lu - ia, al - le - lu - ia.

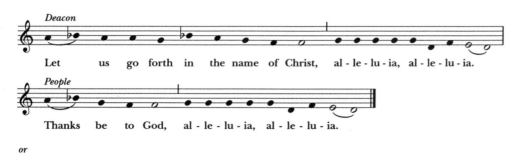

Let us go forth in the name of Christ, al - le - lu - ia, al - le - lu - ia.

Thanks be to God, al - le - lu - ia, al - le - lu - ia.

or

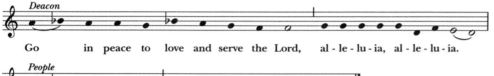

Go in peace to love and serve the Lord, al - le - lu - ia, al - le - lu - ia.

Thanks be to God, al - le - lu - ia, al - le - lu - ia.

or

Let us go forth into the world, rejoicing in the

pow - er of the Spi - rit, al - le - lu - ia, al - le - lu - ia.

Thanks be to God, al - le - lu - ia, al - le - lu - ia.

or the following

Let us bless the Lord, al - le - lu - ia, al - le - lu - ia.

Thanks be to God, al - le - lu - ia, al - le - lu - ia.

Setting: From *Missa orbis factor*; Plainsong, Tonus Peregrinus; adapt. David Hurd (b. 1950)

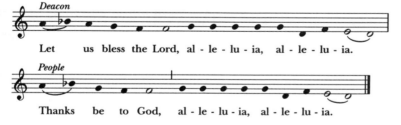

THE HOLY EUCHARIST, RITE II

The Decalogue (S354)

CD II   TRACK 69

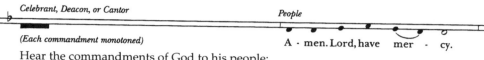

(Each commandment monotoned)

Hear the commandments of God to his people:
I am the Lord your God who brought you out
        of bondage.
You shall have no other gods but me.

Setting: Howard E. Galley (b. 1929)
© 1985, Howard E. Galley Jr.

Opening Acclamations

CD I   *See TRACKS 36,37,38,39,42,43*

Salutation

CD I   *See TRACK 2*

Collect Tones I and II

CD I   *See TRACKS 44-45*

Prayers of the People

CD I   *See TRACKS 49-52*
CD II   *See TRACKS 1-3*

The Peace

CD II   *See TRACK 5*

The Great Thanksgiving

Dialogue (S120)

CD II   TRACK 70

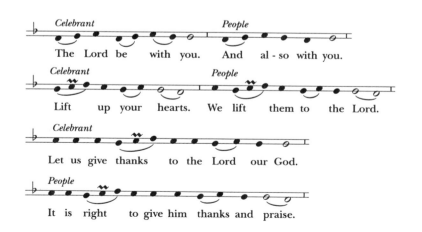

Prefaces Solemn Tone Rite II

The Lord's Day 1 (Of God the Father)

CD II TRACK 71

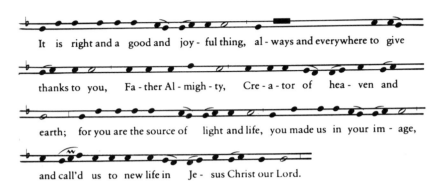

It is right and a good and joy-ful thing, al-ways and everywhere to give thanks to you, Fa-ther Al-migh-ty, Cre-a-tor of hea-ven and earth; for you are the source of light and life, you made us in your im-age, and call'd us to new life in Je-sus Christ our Lord.

The Lord's Day 2 (Of God the Son)

CD II TRACK 72

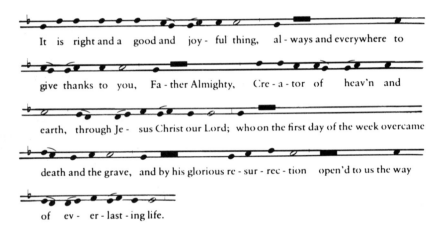

It is right and a good and joy-ful thing, al-ways and everywhere to give thanks to you, Fa-ther Almighty, Cre-a-tor of heav'n and earth, through Je-sus Christ our Lord; who on the first day of the week overcame death and the grave, and by his glorious re-sur-rec-tion open'd to us the way of ev-er-last-ing life.

The Lord's Day 3 (Of God the Holy Spirit)

CD III TRACK 1

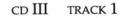

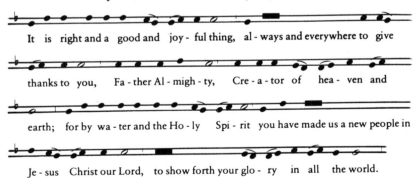

It is right and a good and joy-ful thing, al-ways and everywhere to give thanks to you, Fa-ther Al-migh-ty, Cre-a-tor of hea-ven and earth; for by wa-ter and the Ho-ly Spi-rit you have made us a new people in Je-sus Christ our Lord, to show forth your glo-ry in all the world.

Weekdays after Pentecost

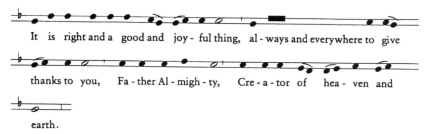

It is right and a good and joy - ful thing, al - ways and everywhere to give

thanks to you, Fa - ther Al - migh - ty, Cre - a - tor of hea - ven and

earth.

Advent

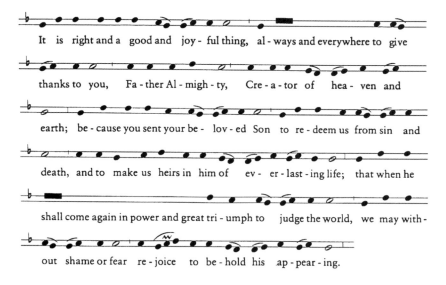

It is right and a good and joy - ful thing, al - ways and everywhere to give

thanks to you, Fa - ther Al - migh - ty, Cre - a - tor of hea - ven and

earth; be - cause you sent your be - lov - ed Son to re - deem us from sin and

death, and to make us heirs in him of ev - er - last - ing life; that when he

shall come again in power and great tri - umph to judge the world, we may with -

out shame or fear re - joice to be - hold his ap - pear - ing.

There - fore we praise you, joining our voices with Angels and Arch - an - gels and

with all the company of hea - ven, who for ev - er sing this hymn to pro -

claim the glo - ry of your Name:

Incarnation

It is right and a good and joy-ful thing, al-ways and everywhere to give

thanks to you, Fa-ther Al-migh-ty, Cre-a-tor of hea-ven and

earth; be-cause you gave Jesus Christ your only Son to be born for us; who,

by the mighty power of the Ho-ly Spi-rit, was made per-fect Man of the

flesh of the Vir-gin Ma-ry his mo-ther; so that we might be deliver'd from

the bon-dage of sin, and re-ceive pow'r to be-come your chil-dren.

Epiphany

It is right and a good and joy-ful thing, al-ways and everywhere to give

thanks to you, Fa-ther Al-migh-ty, Cre-a-tor of hea-ven and

earth; be-cause in the mystery of the Word made flesh, you have caus'd a new

light to shine in our hearts, to give the knowledge of your glo-ry in the face of

your Son Je-sus Christ our Lord.

Lent (1)

It is right and a good and joy-ful thing, al-ways and everywhere to give

thanks to you, Fa-ther Al-migh-ty, Cre-a-tor of hea-ven and

earth, through Je-sus Christ our Lord; who was tempted in every way as we are

yet did not sin. By his grace we are able to triumph over ev-'ry e-vil,

and to live no longer for our-selves a-lone, but for him who died for us

and rose a-gain.

Lent (2)

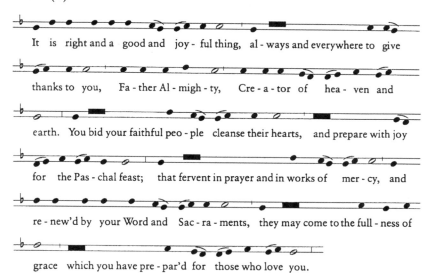

It is right and a good and joy-ful thing, al-ways and everywhere to give thanks to you, Fa-ther Al-migh-ty, Cre-a-tor of hea-ven and earth. You bid your faithful peo-ple cleanse their hearts, and prepare with joy for the Pas-chal feast; that fervent in prayer and in works of mer-cy, and re-new'd by your Word and Sac-ra-ments, they may come to the full-ness of grace which you have pre-par'd for those who love you.

Holy Week

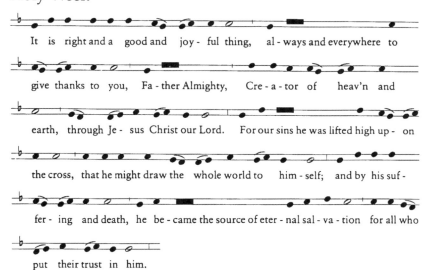

It is right and a good and joy-ful thing, al-ways and everywhere to give thanks to you, Fa-ther Almighty, Cre-a-tor of heav'n and earth, through Je-sus Christ our Lord. For our sins he was lifted high up-on the cross, that he might draw the whole world to him-self; and by his suf-fer-ing and death, he be-came the source of eter-nal sal-va-tion for all who put their trust in him.

There-fore we praise you, joining our voices with Angels and Arch-an-gels and with all the company of hea-ven, who for ev-er sing this hymn to pro-claim the glo-ry of your Name:

Easter

It is right and a good and joy-ful thing, al-ways and everywhere to give thanks to you, Fa-ther Al-migh-ty, Cre-a-tor of hea-ven and earth; but chiefly are we bound to praise you for the glo-rious re-sur-rec-tion of your Son Je-sus Christ our Lord; for he is the true Pas-chal Lamb, who was sac-ri-fic'd for us, and has ta-ken a-way the sin of the world. By his death he has de-stroy'd death, and by his ris-ing to life a-gain he has won for us ev-er-last-ing life.

Ascension

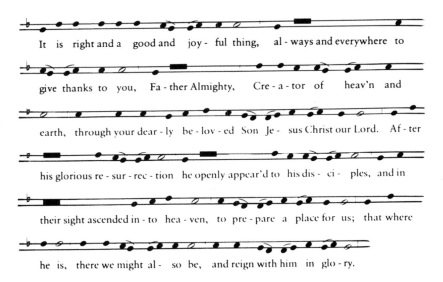

It is right and a good and joy-ful thing, al-ways and everywhere to give thanks to you, Fa-ther Almighty, Cre-a-tor of heav'n and earth, through your dear-ly be-lov-ed Son Je-sus Christ our Lord. Af-ter his glorious re-sur-rec-tion he openly appear'd to his dis-ci-ples, and in their sight ascended in-to hea-ven, to pre-pare a place for us; that where he is, there we might al-so be, and reign with him in glo-ry.

Pentecost

It is right and a good and joy-ful thing, al-ways and everywhere to give thanks to you, Fa-ther Almighty, Cre-a-tor of heav'n and earth, through Je-sus Christ our Lord. In ful-fill-ment of his true pro-mise, the Holy Spirit came down [on this day] from hea-ven, light-ing up-on the dis-ci-ples, to teach them and to lead them in-to all truth; u-niting peoples of many tongues in the con-fess-ion of one faith, and giving to your Church the power to serve you as a roy-al priest-hood, and to preach the Gos-pel to all na-tions.

Trinity Sunday

It is right and a good and joy-ful thing, al-ways and everywhere to give thanks to you, Fa-ther Al-migh-ty, Cre-a-tor of hea-ven and earth; for with your co-eternal Son and Ho-ly Spi-rit, you are one God, one Lord, in Tri-ni-ty of Per-sons and in U-ni-ty of Be-ing; and we celebrate the one and e-qual glo-ry of you, O Fa-ther, and of the Son, and of the Ho-ly Spi-rit.

There-fore we praise you, joining our voices with Angels and Arch-an-gels and with all the company of hea-ven, who for ev-er sing this hymn to pro-claim the glo-ry of your Name:

All Saints

CD III   TRACK 13

It is right and a good and joy-ful thing, al-ways and everywhere to give thanks to you, Fa-ther Al-migh-ty, Cre-a-tor of hea-ven and earth; for in the multitude of your saints you have surrounded us with a great cloud of wit-ness-es, that we might rejoice in their fel-low-ship, and run with en-dur-ance the race that is set be-fore us; and to-gether with them re-ceive the crown of glo-ry that nev-er fades a-way.

A Saint (1)

CD III   TRACK 14

It is right and a good and joy-ful thing, al-ways and everywhere to give thanks to you, Fa-ther Almighty, Cre-a-tor of heav'n and earth, for the won-der-ful grace and vir-tue de-clar'd in all your saints, who have been the cho-sen ves-sels of your grace, and the lights of the world in their ge-ne-ra-tions.

A Saint (2)

CD III   TRACK 15

It is right and a good and joy-ful thing, al-ways and everywhere to give thanks to you, Fa-ther Al-migh-ty, Cre-a-tor of hea-ven and earth; be-cause in the o-be-dience of your saints you have giv-en us an ex-am-ple of right-eous-ness, and in their e-ter-nal joy a glo-rious pledge of the hope of our call-ing.

A Saint (3)

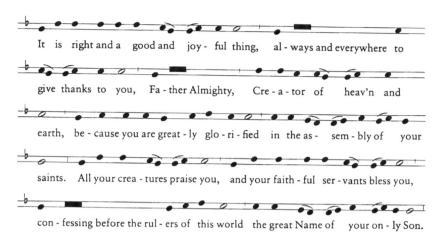

It is right and a good and joy-ful thing, al-ways and everywhere to give thanks to you, Fa-ther Almighty, Cre-a-tor of heav'n and earth, be-cause you are great-ly glo-ri-fied in the as-sem-bly of your saints. All your crea-tures praise you, and your faith-ful ser-vants bless you, con-fessing before the rul-ers of this world the great Name of your on-ly Son.

Apostles and Ordinations

It is right and a good and joy-ful thing, al-ways and everywhere to give thanks to you, Fa-ther Almighty, Cre-a-tor of heav'n and earth, through the great shep-herd of your flock Je-sus Christ our Lord; who after his resurrection sent forth his a-pos-tles to preach the Gos-pel and to teach all na-tions; and pro-mis'd to be with them al-ways, ev-en to the end of the a-ges.

There-fore we praise you, joining our voices with Angels and Arch-an-gels and with all the company of hea-ven, who for ev-er sing this hymn to pro-claim the glo-ry of your Name:

Dedication of a Church

CD III TRACK 18

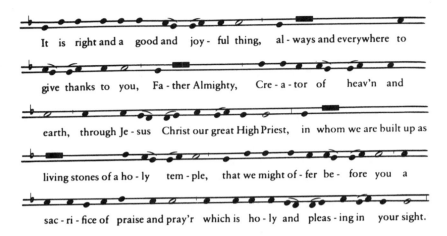

It is right and a good and joy-ful thing, al-ways and everywhere to give thanks to you, Fa-ther Almighty, Cre-a-tor of heav'n and earth, through Je-sus Christ our great High Priest, in whom we are built up as living stones of a ho-ly tem-ple, that we might of-fer be-fore you a sac-ri-fice of praise and pray'r which is ho-ly and pleas-ing in your sight.

Baptism

CD III TRACK 19

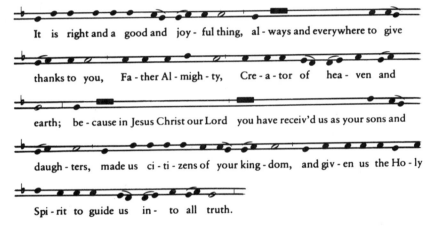

It is right and a good and joy-ful thing, al-ways and everywhere to give thanks to you, Fa-ther Al-migh-ty, Cre-a-tor of hea-ven and earth; be-cause in Jesus Christ our Lord you have receiv'd us as your sons and daugh-ters, made us ci-ti-zens of your king-dom, and giv-en us the Ho-ly Spi-rit to guide us in-to all truth.

Marriage

CD III TRACK 20

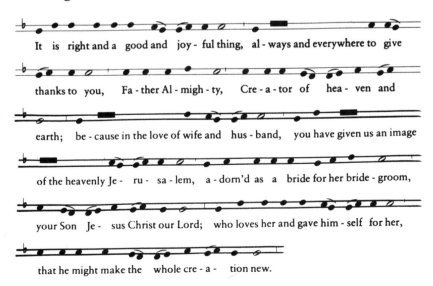

It is right and a good and joy-ful thing, al-ways and everywhere to give thanks to you, Fa-ther Al-migh-ty, Cre-a-tor of hea-ven and earth; be-cause in the love of wife and hus-band, you have given us an image of the heavenly Je-ru-sa-lem, a-dorn'd as a bride for her bride-groom, your Son Je-sus Christ our Lord; who loves her and gave him-self for her, that he might make the whole cre-a-tion new.

Commemoration of the Dead

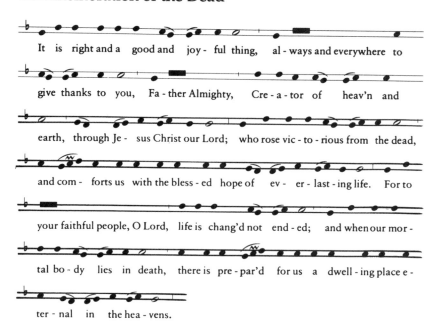

It is right and a good and joy-ful thing, al-ways and everywhere to give thanks to you, Fa-ther Almighty, Cre-a-tor of heav'n and earth, through Je-sus Christ our Lord; who rose vic-to-rious from the dead, and com-forts us with the bless-ed hope of ev-er-last-ing life. For to your faithful people, O Lord, life is chang'd not end-ed; and when our mor-tal bo-dy lies in death, there is pre-par'd for us a dwell-ing place e-ter-nal in the hea-vens.

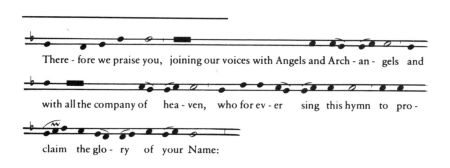

There-fore we praise you, joining our voices with Angels and Arch-an-gels and with all the company of hea-ven, who for ev-er sing this hymn to pro-claim the glo-ry of your Name:

Prefaces Simple Tone Rite II

The Lord's Day 1 (Of God the Father)

CD III   TRACK 22

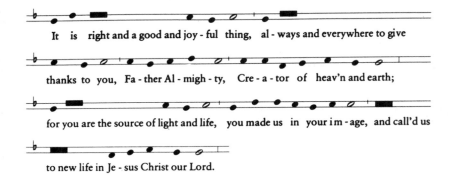

It is right and a good and joy-ful thing, al-ways and everywhere to give thanks to you, Fa-ther Al-migh-ty, Cre-a-tor of heav'n and earth; for you are the source of light and life, you made us in your im-age, and call'd us to new life in Je-sus Christ our Lord.

The Lord's Day 2 (Of God the Son)

CD III   TRACK 23

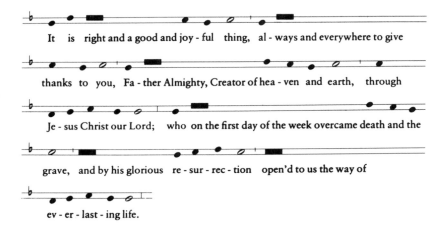

It is right and a good and joy-ful thing, al-ways and everywhere to give thanks to you, Fa-ther Almighty, Creator of hea-ven and earth, through Je-sus Christ our Lord; who on the first day of the week overcame death and the grave, and by his glorious re-sur-rec-tion open'd to us the way of ev-er-last-ing life.

The Lord's Day 3 (Of God the Holy Spirit)

CD III   TRACK 24

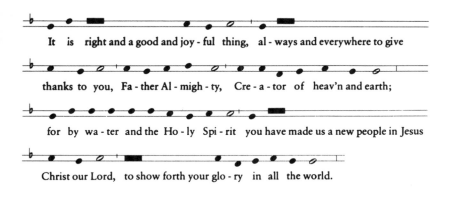

It is right and a good and joy-ful thing, al-ways and everywhere to give thanks to you, Fa-ther Al-migh-ty, Cre-a-tor of heav'n and earth; for by wa-ter and the Ho-ly Spi-rit you have made us a new people in Jesus Christ our Lord, to show forth your glo-ry in all the world.

Weekdays after Pentecost

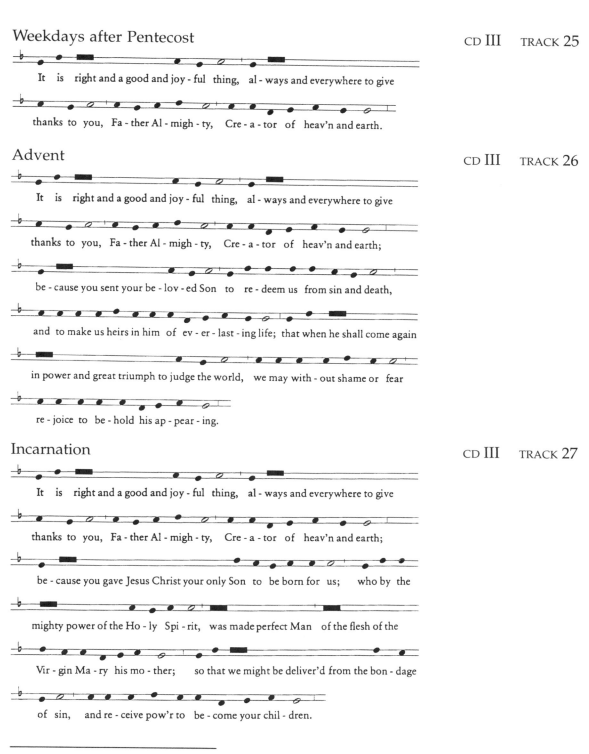

It is right and a good and joy - ful thing,   al - ways and everywhere to give

thanks to you, Fa - ther Al - migh - ty,   Cre - a - tor of heav'n and earth.

Advent

It is right and a good and joy - ful thing,   al - ways and everywhere to give

thanks to you, Fa - ther Al - migh - ty,   Cre - a - tor of heav'n and earth;

be - cause you sent your be - lov - ed Son   to re - deem us from sin and death,

and to make us heirs in him of ev - er - last - ing life;   that when he shall come again

in power and great triumph to judge the world,   we may with - out shame or fear

re - joice to be - hold his ap - pear - ing.

Incarnation

It is right and a good and joy - ful thing,   al - ways and everywhere to give

thanks to you, Fa - ther Al - migh - ty,   Cre - a - tor of heav'n and earth;

be - cause you gave Jesus Christ your only Son   to be born for us;   who by the

mighty power of the Ho - ly Spi - rit,   was made perfect Man   of the flesh of the

Vir - gin Ma - ry his mo - ther;   so that we might be deliver'd from the bon - dage

of sin,   and re - ceive pow'r to be - come your chil - dren.

There - fore we praise you,   joining our voices with Angels and Arch - an - gels

and with all the compa - ny of hea - ven   who for ev - er sing this hymn

to pro - claim the glo - ry of your Name:

Epiphany

It is right and a good and joy - ful thing, al - ways and everywhere to give

thanks to you, Fa - ther Al - migh - ty, Cre - a - tor of heav'n and earth;

be - cause in the mystery of the Word made flesh, you have caus'd a new light to

shine in our hearts, to give the knowledge of your glo - ry in the face of your Son

Je - sus Christ our Lord.

Lent (1)

It is right and a good and joy - ful thing, al - ways and everywhere to give

thanks to you, Fa - ther Al - migh - ty, Cre - a - tor of heav'n and earth;

through Je - sus Christ our Lord; who was tempted in every way as we are yet did

not sin. By his grace we are able to triumph over ev -'ry e - vil, and to live no

longer for our - selves a - lone, but for him who died for us and rose a - gain.

Lent (2)

It is right and a good and joy - ful thing, al - ways and everywhere to give

thanks to you, Fa - ther Al - migh - ty, Cre - a - tor of heav'n and earth.

You bid your faithful people cleanse their hearts, and prepare with joy for the

Pas - chal feast; that fervent in prayer and in works of mer - cy, and re - new'd

by your Word and Sac - ra - ments, they may come to the full - ness of grace

which you have prepar'd for those who love you.

Holy Week

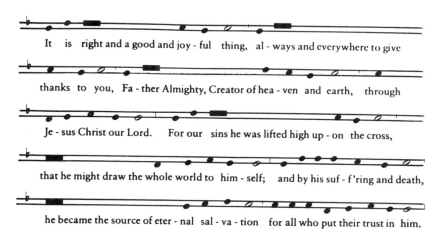

It is right and a good and joy-ful thing, al-ways and everywhere to give

thanks to you, Fa-ther Almighty, Creator of hea-ven and earth, through

Je-sus Christ our Lord.   For our sins he was lifted high up-on the cross,

that he might draw the whole world to him-self;   and by his suf-f'ring and death,

he became the source of eter-nal sal-va-tion for all who put their trust in him.

Easter

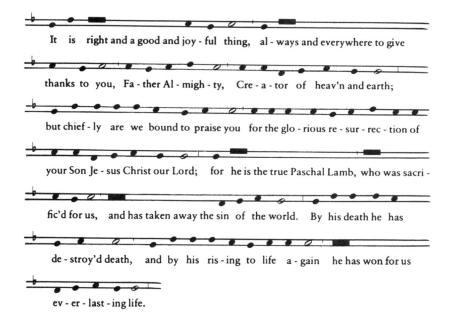

It is right and a good and joy-ful thing, al-ways and everywhere to give

thanks to you, Fa-ther Al-migh-ty, Cre-a-tor of heav'n and earth;

but chief-ly are we bound to praise you for the glo-rious re-sur-rec-tion of

your Son Je-sus Christ our Lord;   for he is the true Paschal Lamb, who was sacri-

fic'd for us,   and has taken away the sin of the world. By his death he has

de-stroy'd death,   and by his ris-ing to life a-gain he has won for us

ev-er-last-ing life.

There-fore we praise you, joining our voices with Angels and Arch-an-gels

and with all the compa-ny of hea-ven who for ev-er sing this hymn

to pro-claim the glo-ry of your Name:

Ascension

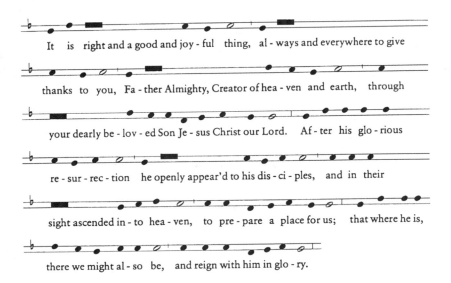

It is right and a good and joy-ful thing, al-ways and everywhere to give thanks to you, Fa-ther Almighty, Creator of hea-ven and earth, through your dearly be-lov-ed Son Je-sus Christ our Lord. Af-ter his glo-rious re-sur-rec-tion he openly appear'd to his dis-ci-ples, and in their sight ascended in-to hea-ven, to pre-pare a place for us; that where he is, there we might al-so be, and reign with him in glo-ry.

Pentecost

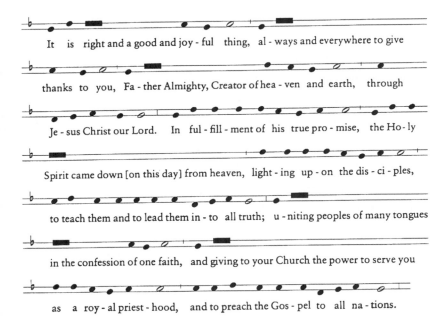

It is right and a good and joy-ful thing, al-ways and everywhere to give thanks to you, Fa-ther Almighty, Creator of hea-ven and earth, through Je-sus Christ our Lord. In ful-fill-ment of his true pro-mise, the Ho-ly Spirit came down [on this day] from heaven, light-ing up-on the dis-ci-ples, to teach them and to lead them in-to all truth; u-niting peoples of many tongues in the confession of one faith, and giving to your Church the power to serve you as a roy-al priest-hood, and to preach the Gos-pel to all na-tions.

Trinity Sunday

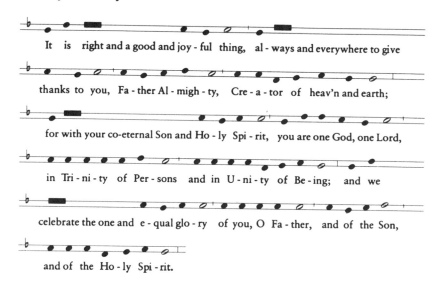

It is right and a good and joy - ful thing, al - ways and everywhere to give

thanks to you, Fa - ther Al - migh - ty, Cre - a - tor of heav'n and earth;

for with your co-eternal Son and Ho - ly Spi - rit, you are one God, one Lord,

in Tri - ni - ty of Per - sons and in U - ni - ty of Be - ing; and we

celebrate the one and e - qual glo - ry of you, O Fa - ther, and of the Son,

and of the Ho - ly Spi - rit.

All Saints

It is right and a good and joy - ful thing, al - ways and everywhere to give

thanks to you, Fa - ther Al - migh - ty, Cre - a - tor of heav'n and earth;

for in the multitude of your saints   you have surrounded us with a great cloud of

wit - ness - es, that we might re - joice in their fel - low - ship,   and run with en -

dur - ance the race that is set be - fore us;   and to - gether with them receive the

crown of glo - ry   that nev - er fades a - way.

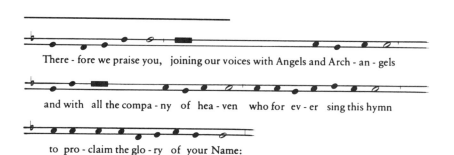

There - fore we praise you, joining our voices with Angels and Arch - an - gels

and with all the compa - ny of hea - ven who for ev - er sing this hymn

to pro - claim the glo - ry of your Name:

A Saint (1)

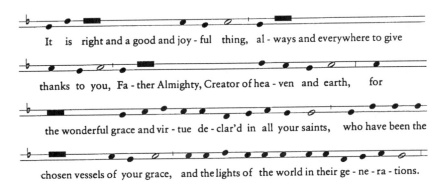

It is right and a good and joy-ful thing, al-ways and everywhere to give thanks to you, Fa-ther Almighty, Creator of hea-ven and earth, for the wonderful grace and vir-tue de-clar'd in all your saints, who have been the chosen vessels of your grace, and the lights of the world in their ge-ne-ra-tions.

A Saint (2)

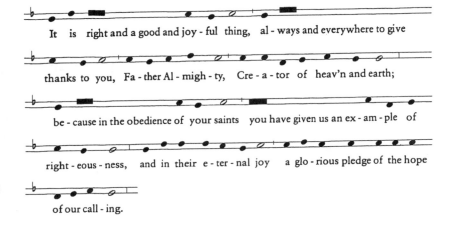

It is right and a good and joy-ful thing, al-ways and everywhere to give thanks to you, Fa-ther Al-migh-ty, Cre-a-tor of heav'n and earth; be-cause in the obedience of your saints you have given us an ex-am-ple of right-eous-ness, and in their e-ter-nal joy a glo-rious pledge of the hope of our call-ing.

A Saint (3)

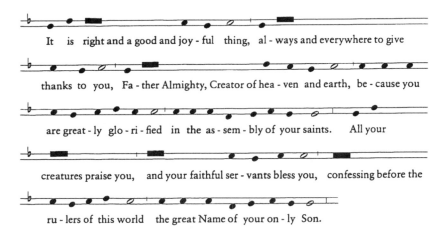

It is right and a good and joy-ful thing, al-ways and everywhere to give thanks to you, Fa-ther Almighty, Creator of hea-ven and earth, be-cause you are great-ly glo-ri-fied in the as-sem-bly of your saints. All your creatures praise you, and your faithful ser-vants bless you, confessing before the ru-lers of this world the great Name of your on-ly Son.

Apostles and Ordinations

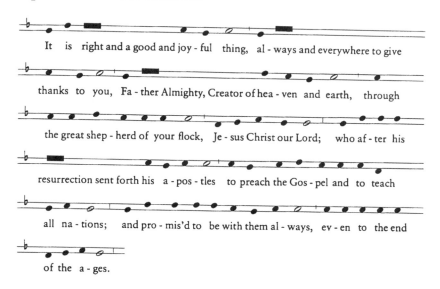

It is right and a good and joy-ful thing, al-ways and everywhere to give

thanks to you, Fa-ther Almighty, Creator of hea-ven and earth, through

the great shep-herd of your flock, Je-sus Christ our Lord; who af-ter his

resurrection sent forth his a-pos-tles to preach the Gos-pel and to teach

all na-tions; and pro-mis'd to be with them al-ways, ev-en to the end

of the a-ges.

Dedication of a Church

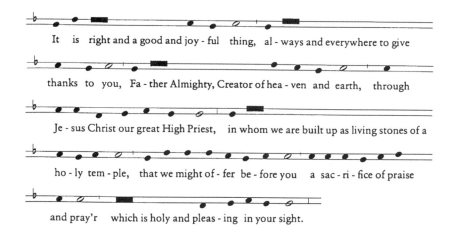

It is right and a good and joy-ful thing, al-ways and everywhere to give

thanks to you, Fa-ther Almighty, Creator of hea-ven and earth, through

Je-sus Christ our great High Priest, in whom we are built up as living stones of a

ho-ly tem-ple, that we might of-fer be-fore you a sac-ri-fice of praise

and pray'r which is holy and pleas-ing in your sight.

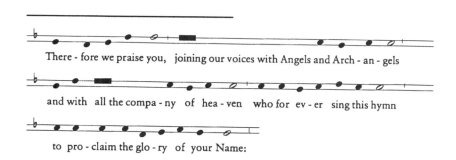

There-fore we praise you, joining our voices with Angels and Arch-an-gels

and with all the compa-ny of hea-ven who for ev-er sing this hymn

to pro-claim the glo-ry of your Name:

Baptism

It is right and a good and joy-ful thing, al-ways and everywhere to give

thanks to you, Fa-ther Al-migh-ty, Cre-a-tor of heav'n and earth;

be-cause in Jesus Christ our Lord you have receiv'd us as your sons and daugh-

ters, made us ci-ti-zens of your king-dom, and giv-en us the Ho-ly Spi-rit

to guide us in-to all truth.

Marriage

It is right and a good and joy-ful thing, al-ways and everywhere to give

thanks to you, Fa-ther Al-migh-ty, Cre-a-tor of heav'n and earth;

be-cause in the love of wife and hus-band, you have given us an image

of the heaven-ly Je-ru-sa-lem, a-dorn'd as a bride for her bride-groom,

your Son Je-sus Christ our Lord; who loves her and gave him-self for her,

that he might make the whole Cre-a-tion new.

Commemoration of the Dead

It is right and a good and joy-ful thing, al-ways and everywhere to give

thanks to you, Fa-ther Almighty, Creator of hea-ven and earth, through

Je-sus Christ our Lord; who rose victorious from the dead, and com-forts us

with the bless-ed hope of ev-er-last-ing life. For to your faithful people,

O Lord, life is chang'd not end-ed; and when our mortal body lies in death,

there is pre-par'd for us a dwell-ing place e-ter-nal in the hea-vens.

Conclusion of the Eucharistic Prayer Rite II

Solemn Tone Prayer A

CD III   TRACK 45

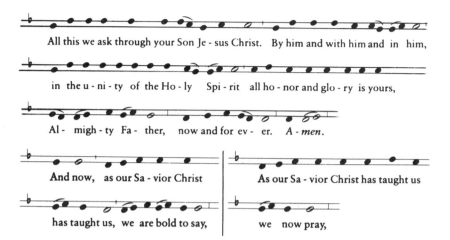

All this we ask through your Son Je - sus Christ. By him and with him and in him,

in the u - ni - ty of the Ho - ly Spi - rit all ho - nor and glo - ry is yours,

Al - migh - ty Fa - ther, now and for ev - er. A - men.

And now, as our Sa - vior Christ   As our Sa - vior Christ has taught us

has taught us, we are bold to say,   we now pray,

Simple Tone Prayer A

CD III   TRACK 46

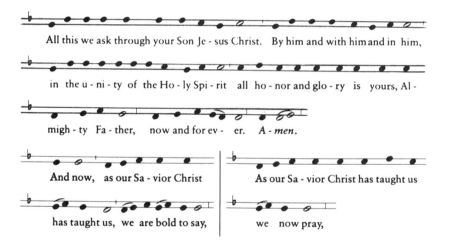

All this we ask through your Son Je - sus Christ. By him and with him and in him,

in the u - ni - ty of the Ho - ly Spi - rit all ho - nor and glo - ry is yours, Al -

migh - ty Fa - ther, now and for ev - er. A - men.

And now, as our Sa - vior Christ   As our Sa - vior Christ has taught us

has taught us, we are bold to say,   we now pray,

Solemn Tone Prayer B

CD III   TRACK 47

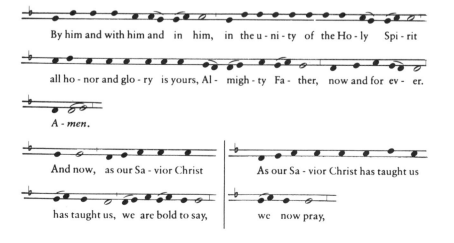

By him and with him and in him, in the u - ni - ty of the Ho - ly Spi - rit

all ho - nor and glo - ry is yours, Al - migh - ty Fa - ther, now and for ev - er.

A - men.

And now, as our Sa - vior Christ   As our Sa - vior Christ has taught us

has taught us, we are bold to say,   we now pray,

Simple Tone Prayer B

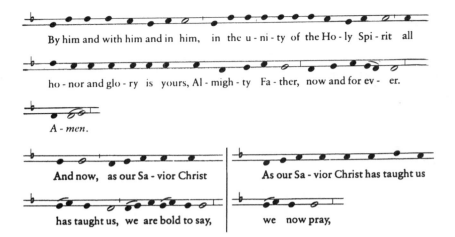

By him and with him and in him, in the u - ni - ty of the Ho - ly Spi - rit all

ho - nor and glo - ry is yours, Al - migh - ty Fa - ther, now and for ev - er.

A - men.

And now, as our Sa - vior Christ   As our Sa - vior Christ has taught us

has taught us, we are bold to say,   we   now pray,

Solemn Tone Prayer C

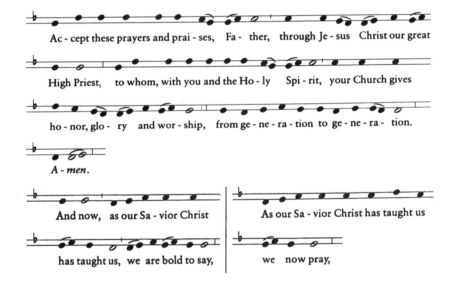

Ac - cept these prayers and prai - ses, Fa - ther, through Je - sus Christ our great

High Priest,   to whom, with you and the Ho - ly   Spi - rit, your Church gives

ho - nor, glo - ry   and wor - ship, from ge - ne - ra - tion to ge - ne - ra - tion.

A - men.

And now, as our Sa - vior Christ   As our Sa - vior Christ has taught us

has taught us, we are bold to say,   we   now pray,

Simple Tone Prayer C

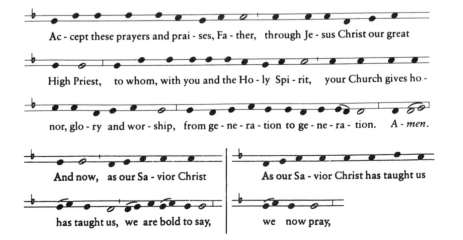

Ac - cept these prayers and prai - ses, Fa - ther, through Je - sus Christ our great

High Priest,   to whom, with you and the Ho - ly Spi - rit,   your Church gives ho -

nor, glo - ry and wor - ship, from ge - ne - ra - tion to ge - ne - ra - tion.   A - men.

And now, as our Sa - vior Christ   As our Sa - vior Christ has taught us

has taught us, we are bold to say,   we   now pray,

Prayer C (S120, S369)

Celebrant: The Lord be with you. **People:** And also with you.

Celebrant: Lift up your hearts. **People:** We lift them to the Lord.

Celebrant: Let us give thanks to the Lord our God.

People: It is right to give him thanks and praise.

Celebrant: God of all power, Ruler of the Universe, you are worthy of

glory and praise.

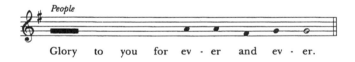

People: Glory to you for ever and ever.

Celebrant: At your command all things came to be: the vast expanse of inter

stellar space, galaxies, suns, the planets in their courses,

and this fragile earth, our island home.

People

By your will they were cre-a-ted and have their be-ing.

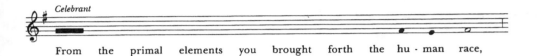

Celebrant

From the primal elements you brought forth the hu-man race,

and blessed us with memory, rea-son, and skill. You made us the rulers

of cre-a-tion. But we turned against you, and be-trayed your trust,

and we turned against one an-oth-er.

People

Have mercy, Lord, for we are sin-ners in your sight.

Celebrant

Again and again, you called us to re-turn. Through prophets and

sages you revealed your right-eous Law. And in the fullness of time

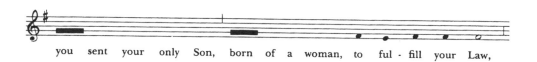

you sent your only Son, born of a woman, to ful-fill your Law,

to open for us the way of free-dom and peace.

People

By his blood, he reconciled us. By his wounds, we are healed.

Celebrant

And therefore we praise you, joining with the hea-ven-ly cho-rus,

with prophets, apos-tles, and mar-tyrs, and with all those in every

generation who have looked to you in hope, to proclaim with

them your glo-ry, in their un-end-ing hymn:

Here is sung a setting of "Holy, holy, holy Lord."

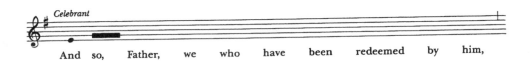

And so, Father, we who have been redeemed by him,

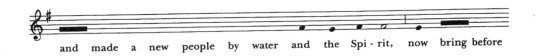

and made a new people by water and the Spi-rit, now bring before

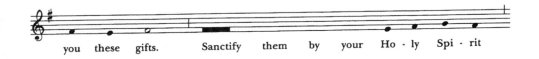

you these gifts. Sanctify them by your Ho-ly Spi-rit

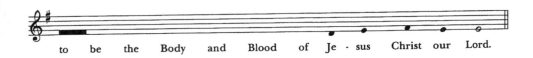

to be the Body and Blood of Je-sus Christ our Lord.

On the night he was betrayed, he took bread, said the blessing,

broke the bread, and gave it to his friends, and said, "Take, eat:

This is my Body, which is giv - en for you. Do this for the re -

mem - brance of me." Af - ter supper, he took the cup of wine,

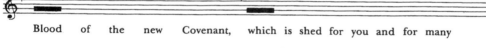

gave thanks, and said, "Drink this, all of you: This is my

Blood of the new Covenant, which is shed for you and for many

for the forgive - ness of sins. Whenever you drink it,

do this for the re - mem - brance of me.

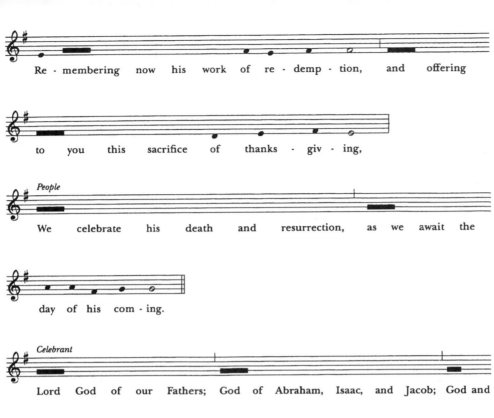

Re - membering now his work of re - demp - tion, and offering

to you this sacrifice of thanks - giv - ing,

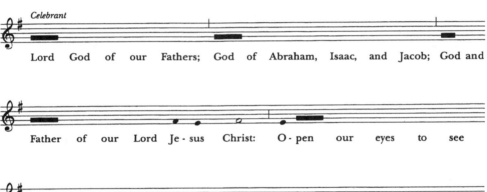

People

We celebrate his death and resurrection, as we await the

day of his com - ing.

Celebrant

Lord God of our Fathers; God of Abraham, Isaac, and Jacob; God and

Father of our Lord Je - sus Christ: O - pen our eyes to see

your hand at work in the world a - bout us. De - liver us from the

presumption of coming to this Ta - ble for solace only, and

not for strength; for pardon only, and not for re - new - al.

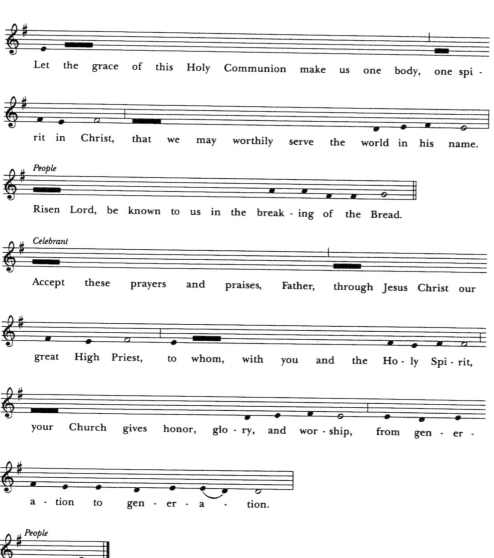

Let the grace of this Holy Communion make us one body, one spi-rit in Christ, that we may worthily serve the world in his name.

People

Risen Lord, be known to us in the break-ing of the Bread.

Celebrant

Accept these prayers and praises, Father, through Jesus Christ our great High Priest, to whom, with you and the Ho-ly Spi-rit, your Church gives honor, glo-ry, and wor-ship, from gen-er-a-tion to gen-er-a-tion.

People

A-men.

Setting: Simple Preface Tone with Responses; adapt. Howard E. Galley (b. 1929)
© 1985, Howard Galley, Jr.

Prayer D Mozarabic Preface

CD III   TRACK 52

Celebrant The Lord be with you. *People* And al-so with you.

Celebrant Lift up your hearts. *People* We lift them to the Lord.

Celebrant Let us give thanks to the Lord our God.

People It is right to give him thanks and praise.

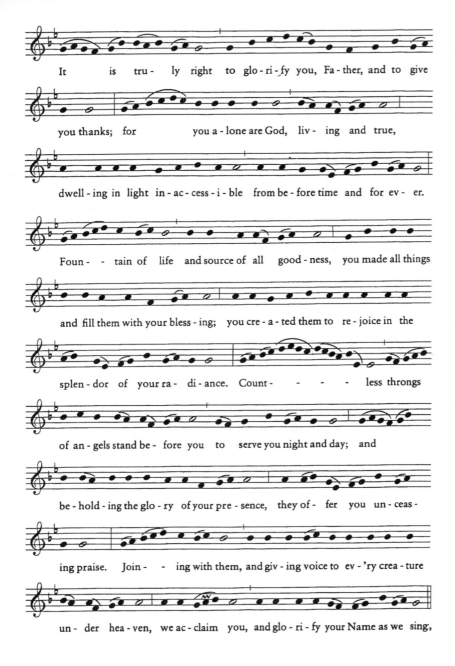

It is tru - ly right to glo-ri-fy you, Fa-ther, and to give

you thanks; for you a - lone are God, liv - ing and true,

dwell - ing in light in - ac - cess - i - ble from be - fore time and for ev - er.

Foun - - tain of life and source of all good - ness, you made all things

and fill them with your bless - ing; you cre - a - ted them to re - joice in the

splen - dor of your ra - di - ance. Count - - - - less throngs

of an - gels stand be - fore you to serve you night and day; and

be - hold - ing the glo - ry of your pre - sence, they of - fer you un - ceas -

ing praise. Join - - ing with them, and giv - ing voice to ev - 'ry crea - ture

un - der hea - ven, we ac - claim you, and glo - ri - fy your Name as we sing,

Mozarabic Conclusion of the Prayer

CD III   TRACK 53

Through Christ and with Christ and in Christ, all ho - nor and glo - ry are

yours, Al - migh - ty God and Fa - ther, in the u - ni - ty of the

Ho - ly Spi - rit, for ev - er and ev - er. A - men.

Solemn Tone Preface, Conclusion of the Prayer, and Introduction
to the Lord's Prayer, traditional and contemporary

CD III   TRACK 54

It is truly right to glorify you, Father, and to give you thanks; for you alone are God, liv-ing and true, dwell-ing in light in-ac-cess-i-ble from be-fore time and for ev-er. Foun-tain of life and source of all good-ness, you made all things and fill them with your bless-ing; you cre-a-ted them to re-joice in the splen-dor of your ra-diance. Count-less throngs of angels stand be-fore you to serve you night and day; and be-hold-ing the glo-ry of your pre-sence, they of-fer you un-ceas-ing praise. Join-ing with them, and giving voice to every creature un-der hea-ven, we ac-claim you, and glo-ri-fy your Name as we sing,

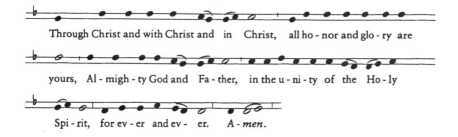

Through Christ and with Christ and in Christ, all ho-nor and glo-ry are yours, Al-migh-ty God and Fa-ther, in the u-ni-ty of the Ho-ly Spi-rit, for ev-er and ev-er. A-men.

And now, as our Sa-vior Christ has taught us, we are bold to say,

As our Sa-vior Christ has taught us we now pray,

107

Invitation to Communion	CD II	*See TRACKS 60-61*
Blessings	CD II	*See TRACKS 62-67*
Dismissals	CD II	*See TRACKS 68-70*

ENRICHING OUR WORSHIP

## Opening Acclamation 1	CD III	TRACK 55

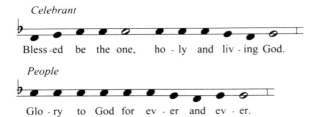

Celebrant

Bless-ed be the one, ho - ly and liv - ing God.

People

Glo - ry to God for ev - er and ev - er.

## Opening Acclamation 2	CD III	TRACK 56

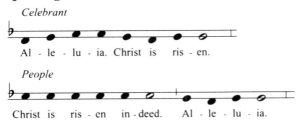

Celebrant

Al - le - lu - ia. Christ is ris - en.

People

Christ is ris - en in - deed. Al - le - lu - ia.

## Opening Acclamation 3	CD III	TRACK 57

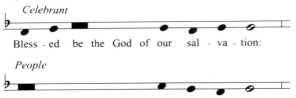

Celebrant

Bless - ed be the God of our sal - va - tion:

People

Who bears our burdens and for - gives our sins.

It is truly right, and good and joy - ful, to give you thanks,

all - ho - ly God, source of life and foun-tain of mer - cy.

You have filled us and all creation with your blessing and fed

us with your con - stant love; you have redeemed us in

Jesus Christ and knit us in - to one bo - dy. Through your Spir - it

you re - plen-ish us and call us to full - ness of life.

There - fore, join - ing with An - gels and Arch - an - gels

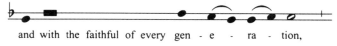

and with the faithful of every gen - e - ra - tion,

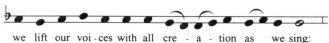

we lift our voi - ces with all cre - a - tion as we sing:

Through Christ and with Christ and in Christ, in the

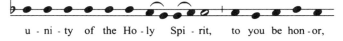

u - ni - ty of the Ho - ly Spi - rit, to you be hon - or,

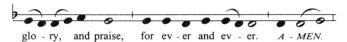

glo - ry, and praise, for ev - er and ev - er. A - MEN.

Chant adaptation by Bruce E. Ford, 1992.

Eucharistic Prayer 2 Preface and concluding Doxology

We praise you and we bless you, ho-ly and gra-cious God,

source of life a-bun-dant. From be-fore time you made

ready the cre-a-tion. Your Spirit moved over the deep

and brought all things in-to be-ing: sun, moon, and stars;

earth, winds, and wa-ters; and ev-'ry liv-ing thing.

You made us in your image, male and fe-male, and taught

us to walk in your ways. But we rebelled against you, and

wan-dered far a-way; and yet, as a mother cares for her

children, you would not for-get us. Time and a-gain

you called us to live in the full-ness of your love.

And so this day we join with Saints and An-gels

in the chorus of praise that rings through e-ter-ni-ty,

lift-ing our voi-ces to mag-ni-fy you as we sing:

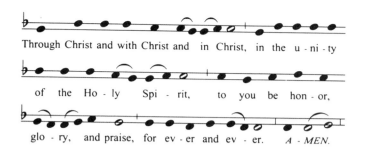

Through Christ and with Christ and in Christ, in the u - ni - ty

of the Ho - ly Spi - rit, to you be hon - or,

glo - ry, and praise, for ev - er and ev - er. *A - MEN*.

Eucharistic Prayer 3 Preface and concluding Doxology

CD III   TRACK 60

All thanks and praise are yours at all times and in all pla - ces,

our true and lov - ing God; through Je - sus Christ, your

e - ter - nal Word, the Wis - dom from on high by whom you

cre - at - ed all things. You laid the foun - da - tions

of the world and en - closed the sea when it burst out of

the womb; You brought forth all crea - tures of the earth

and gave breath to hu - man - kind. Won - drous are you,

Ho - ly One of Bless - ing, all you cre - ate is a sign

of hope for our jour - ney; and so as the morn - ing

stars sing your prai - ses we join the heav - en - ly be - ings

and all cre - a - tion as we shout with joy:

Presider

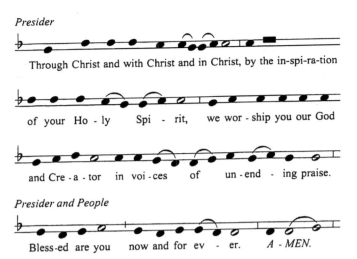

Through Christ and with Christ and in Christ, by the in-spi-ra-tion

of your Ho - ly   Spi - rit,   we wor - ship you our God

and Cre -a - tor   in voi -ces   of   un -end - ing praise.

Presider and People

Bless-ed are you   now and for ev - er.   *A - MEN.*

Fraction Anthem 1

CD **III**   TRACK 61

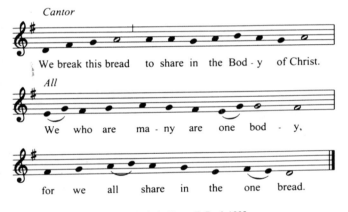

Cantor

We break this bread   to share in the Bod - y   of Christ.

All

We   who are   ma - ny   are   one bod - y,

for   we   all   share   in   the   one   bread.

Centonized Mode 7 antiphon melody by Bruce E. Ford, 1992.